SECULAR CHRIST
A Contemporary Interpretation of Jesus

JOHN J. VINCENT

2890

LUTTERWORTH PRESS · LONDON

First published in Great Britain 1968

Copyright © 1968 *by John J. Vincent*

7188 1387 1

PRINTED IN GREAT BRITAIN
PHOTOLITHO BY EBENEZER BAYLIS AND SON LTD.
THE TRINITY PRESS, WORCESTER, AND LONDON

For
JAMES STAFFORD VINCENT

On His Baptism by His Father-in-law
January 22, 1967

There is no such thing as a "safe" theology.
All theology which is earnest is also dangerous.
It is an act of adoration fraught with the risk of
blasphemy.

EDITORIAL ON PAUL TILLICH

Expository Times, LXIV, 11

PREFACE

This volume is a contribution to the debate among New Testament scholars as to the meaning of the Gospels. It is also a contribution to the more general contemporary debate as to the nature of Christianity itself.

Inevitably, the drift and direction of the book derive from these two preoccupations. Over the past few years these themes have more and more involved my attention, and I would like to record here how much I have gained from the friendly comments of people who have heard me speak in sundry places on these matters. I recall with special pleasure a number of occasions when material contained here was first tried out. These include lectures on "Conversion in a Secular Age" at the World Council of Churches–World Student Christian Federation Consultation at Lincoln in April, 1965; on "The Synoptic Jesus and the Search for a Secular Christianity" at the Oxford Congress for New Testament Studies in September, 1965; on "Secular Society or Secular Christ?" at the Christian Education Movement Conference in December, 1966; and on "Secular Christ" at the Manchester University Extra-Mural Department, January-February, 1967.

On the New Testament side of the matter, this volume represents the end product of a number of experimental articles, more or less all of which must have appeared angular as isolated statements. I have occasionally used paragraphs from these earlier efforts here.[1]

The urgency which seemed to belong to completing the present book has inevitably postponed still further the appearance of the study of discipleship in the Synoptic Gospels, upon which I have been engaged, in what time I could spare, for the past thirteen years. I have not drawn upon that study here, nor yet would I say that my work in that area would inevitably lead to the conclusions here offered. The present work belongs more to the area of speculative New Testament theology than to that of New Testament criticism in its stricter sense. Although, naturally, this book could not have been written without the background of the more meticulous work on individual texts and on wider matters necessary for the other work, I have not, I think, made the appreciation of the argument of this book dependent upon evidence which is not here given. Meanwhile, a few indications of one or two of the directions of my work on discipleship, at least as it applies to the New Testament notions of church and ministry, can be gathered from a recent short study.[2]

Some readers, accustomed to critical writing on the Gospels,

---

[1] "Discipleship and Synoptic Studies," *Theologische Zeitschrift*, XVI (1960), 456-69; "Did Jesus Teach His Disciples to Learn by Heart?" *Studia Evangelica III: Texte und Untersuchungen* (Berlin: Akademie-Verlag, 1964), LXXXVIII, 105-18; "New Bottles or New Wine?" *London Quarterly and Holborn Review*, October, 1964, pp. 299-309; "Markusevangelium," *Biblisch-historisches Handwörterbuch* (Göttingen: Vandenhoeck & Ruprecht, 1964), XI, 1153-56; "Secularisation," *Study Encounter*, II (1966), 43-47.

[2] *The Working Christ: Christ's Ministries through his Church in the New Testament and in the Modern City*. (London: Epworth Press, 1968), 7-18.

may feel that too scant attention is paid to detailed discussion of the authenticity or inauthenticity of statements or reports. Others may feel that I have sidestepped the problem of the historicity of what the Gospels describe in apparently naïve historical terms. In fact, I am fully aware of these problems, and in teaching the study of the Gospels, I do submit each text and each section to this kind of analysis. In writing this book, however, I was so grasped by the mystery, singularity, and mutual consistency of some of the things which Mark (above all) had to say—and the significance of some of the things he did not say—that I wished to expose others to the freshness and theological depth of the Gospels' hints at solving the insolvable. How this relates to the work of other biblical theologians will emerge from chapter 4 and from the whole book. There was simply not room to go into a longer statement of my "critical principles." I am not sure that scholars ought to have such—but there is a long introduction in *Disciple and Lord* which attempts the task of going "Beyond Form Criticism."

As originally written, this book contained a fourth part, entitled "Christ our Contemporary," in which the theme of "The Dynamics of Christ" was worked out in relation to contemporary discussion on human existence, morality, society, and politics. Discussion with friends—above all, a percipient Abingdon Press reader—convinced me that the book stood better as an attempt at the single problem of the reinterpretation of Jesus. If the case here advanced concerning the essential secularity of Jesus be conceded, then part of the proof of the argument will depend upon how the fivefold "dynamics of Christ" actually work out in practical terms. Here I have been greatly stimulated by Paul Lehmann, Harvey Cox, and the discussions in the World Council of Churches on church and society and those within the Prague Christian Peace Conference. I have already

11

made some forays in this area, though I am conscious that my attempts so far to engage christological categories in political, economic, and sociological discussions require a good deal more working out than they have so far received.[3] I hope before too long to supply the material in more detail under the title "The Dynamics of Christ."

The implications of the present book in relation to church practice have also been all but entirely set aside. Obviously, the essential secularity of Christ must demand a new kind of life in the church.

This is particularly true of the church's liturgy, which, on the present argument, must become the place where the small group of the disciples of Jesus act out and repeat the deeds and words of Jesus, so that they may be inspired to the Jesus-deeds of prophecy and action in the world. This involves a rather elaborate liturgical argument, in which attention must be paid to more traditional assessments of the meaning of Christian liturgy. My work on this demands only periods of quiet which I cannot at present foresee in order to get it into its final form. The volume will probably be entitled "Christ and a Living Liturgy."

On more general matters of church life, I have said nothing here. The reader may rightly infer from my twelve years of occupation in mission in the industrial northwest that I regard the most decisive battles facing the church at this moment to be not only intellectual ones, but rather intellectual and practical ones, in the service of a new form of Christ in the world.[4] The church obviously stands judged

[3] *Christ in a Nuclear World* (Nyack, N. Y.: Fellowship Publications, 1962); *Christian Nuclear Perspective* (London: Epworth Press, 1964); "Christ's Ministry and Our Discipleship," in *Biblical Realism Confronts the Nation*, ed. Paul Peachey (Fellowship Publications, 1963), pp. 184-213; "The Way Ahead: Between Protest and Politics," in *Peace on Earth: The Way Ahead*, ed. Walter Stein (New York: Sheed and Ward, 1966), pp. 240-60.

[4] Cf. my *Christ and Methodism: Towards a New Christianity for a New Age* (Nashville: Abingdon Press, 1965).

in the light of the "whole Christ" whom I shall attempt to portray in this book. But the discovery of the church's present tasks goes hand in hand with the discovery of the present Christ. Much talk in high places of the secularity of the gospel—and no sheer and bloody commitment to it in the only place where the mysteries of the secular Christ may be set forth, rehearsed, and openly encountered—will rightly evoke the contempt and condemnation of the world, humanists or otherwise. All that I have written stands against the background of the one word given to our generation —commitment; and that for us means the attempt to battle with the problems "from the inside." A church which must increasingly in our day live without all "props" save those of Christ himself desperately needs not only new ideas, but solid commitment and action in the urban and suburban situations in which we are now, and must increasingly be, engaged in new ways.

It is quite impossible to record how much this book owes to my wife, Grace, who not only schemed endlessly to secure hours when it could be written, but also typed it all out in the family holiday of summer, 1966. My friends Ian Yates and Stuart Jordan greatly helped by work on the Index.

John J. Vincent

Champness Hall, Rochdale
Summer, 1967

CONTENTS

PROLOGUE

The Crisis in the Church and the Survival of Christ

Much of the so-called "radical" writing in the church today seems to assume that the main difficulty is that the church has somehow got "out of touch" with the world, and that it must find a new language, new structures, and new methods whereby the Christian message can become relevant in our day. The current debates about hermeneutics and apologetics, the studies of the "missionary structure" of congregations, and the search for more relevant evangelism engage a great deal of the time of those who are "forward-looking."

Unfortunately, all these things, related though they certainly are to any reformation, have always been the fruits of change rather than the causes of change. In Christian history "the world"—or the Spirit speaking through the world—has always been one side of the crisis-situation. But there has also been a far more important element, intrinsic to Christianity itself. There has also been a radical discovery of some new aspect of the mystery of Christ.

Even at the level of "the world" and its demands, the logic of the contemporary situation is resisted by many in the radical camp. Attitudes, situations, expectations dependent on a time when it could be said with some degree of truth that Christianity was "the religion of the country" are still to be found in the most unexpected places. The logic of disestablishment in the churches of western Europe is clear in a secular, non-churchgoing, humanistic age. But the logic that established churches be helped out of their absurd and embarrassing situation as quickly as possible, so that the world may be confronted at any rate with a semblance of authenticity in the church, is likely to be fiercely resisted.

Above all, in this day, the Christian cause needs to secure its own *self-authenticity*. The days of its "successes" are past. The days of its widespread influence are over. The tactic of throwing in our lot with the forces of secularism might have been relevant fifty years ago. But now it is too late. The forces of secularism are too strong for us. And it is not going to make the slightest difference in the way secular society goes whether or not there are Christians "involved at every point in it"; we haven't enough to go around, in any case, and in the future we shall have fewer still.

In this context the typical behavior of the modern, educated Christian is all too understandable—but ultimately disastrous. Because of the industry of his churchgoing parents, he "gets on" and keeps to his studies. He talks madly about religion and humanism at the university, gets a job from the careers office, and sets out to become the "new class" of the educated, the "meritocrat" of our secular world. In so doing, he settles down in comfortable metropolitan suburbia, and very soon outgrows the pettifogging local congregation of fellow Christians. If he gets ordained, he seeks to ensure that this makes as little difference to his behavior as possible. He becomes an avid reader of detective novels. His "religion" becomes more and more an embarrassment at the points where he has to continue the peculiar traditions within the ecclesiastical framework, and less and less meaningful at the points where, believing Christianity to be humanism, he gets on with the absorbing business of "real life." If he can make it, he leaves the pastorate to teach religion in a school, or goes into broadcasting or lecturing. The churches are left to those who have not sufficient intelligence to get a better job or to find more successful and productive avenues for their endeavor.

To this, all we can say is that the mysteries of Jesus will not survive, much less be plumbed, if the points at which the educated Christian "comes alive" are the mysteries of crime detection, and if the ecclesiastical hocus-pocus is left to rot in its own juice. If there are not mysteries enough "hid with Christ in God," then the whole game is up, and no *rapprochement* with humanism (an embarrassment to the honest humanists in any case!) can or should postpone the day when the Jesus-events are relegated to the categories of myths and historical mistakes.

Much modern criticism of the church and of Christianity is already twenty years out of date. This is particularly true of the humanistic superiority complex, the always-better-than-the-church attitude, the superficial ridiculing of the figure of Christ which one reads so frequently in the frantically avant-garde journalism of the religious writings of the British press. All this is based upon the assumption that Christianity is a kind of establishment position which needs to be knocked down, that the figure of Christ is some "sacred cow" that needs to be destroyed, that Christian doctrine is some sordid joke that needs to be exposed.

There is nothing wrong with this, except that the only position from which the operation can take place is the position the critics so studiously avoid—the position and standpoint of Jesus. God is whittling down his church. The old establishments are ended. Churches still in establishment positions must be hastily rescued out of them. All this will happen. But it will happen in the name of a larger and more universal conception of Jesus. It will not happen in the name of anti-theological humanism, whether or not the writers of it also attend Christian churches. Of course, Christianity has been idiotic, Jesus a curiosity, Christian doctrine a vast game. What we have to discover is whether there is anything else there, and if so, what it is. Otherwise, with relief and without regret, the Christians must say the game is up, and they will say the game is up *in the name of Jesus*. He above all was no supporter of idiotic establishments, status Christologies, or impossible doctrines. So that if it all ends, it will be he, and not the humanists, who ends it. The only possible alternative to an honest suicide is the belief that there is and always was something else in Jesus.

This book is written because its author believes that there is, indeed, and always was, something else in Jesus—something else beside the traditional assessments. Inevitably, this means some kind of survey of where, at the moment, the contemporary debates have landed us. Part I does this, but only with reference to the picture of Jesus argued or assumed by the various writers. The main part of the book is concerned with a reexamination of the Gospel evidences concerning Jesus. The book stands or falls by this reexamination. Part III does no more than seek to develop fragments of a systematic theology, based on the case made from the Gospel evidence.

Only when this prior question about the nature of Christianity itself has been settled, or at least reopened in a new way, is there any point in asking how in the modern world Christianity can be conveyed, received, or lived. I do in fact believe that the coming of secularization is, as Charles Davis has put it, a veritable *kairos* for the church, in that an open, secular, and pluralist society "offers the best chance of carrying out the Christian mission." [1] But I also believe that the pragmatic (not necessarily materialistic) spirit of the secular world offers a new telescope through which part of the essential Christian mysteries can come alive in a new way in our time. Hence, I claim that the question about the survival of Jesus in a world which does not want him means that it is time for the church to ask itself radically who Jesus is. Similarly, the moment of truth facing the theologians at this time is this: Can you stand only in Christ? Beyond this, there is the question about the *meaning* of Christ. But before that is even opened, the absolutely central and sufficient nature of the question about Christ must be asserted.

Christian theology is currently tempted in a variety of directions. To begin with, however much this may appear as a curiosity or as mere antiquarianism to those outside, there is the very considerable weight of traditional theological attitudes. This weight is to be found within the confessional theologies of all churches. Even more significant, in an ecumenical age, is the emergence of attitudes which are easily explicable on confessional grounds into the arena and dignity of systematic theology. Karl Barth can only be understood in the light of Calvin and the church history of the first half of this century; Rudolf Bultmann, I shall suggest, is to be seen first and foremost as a Lutheran; John Macquarrie, to give only one recent example, has to be seen as the Calvinist converted to Anglo-Catholicism. It is not impossible that some of the things I shall say will prove un-

---

[1] *God's Grace in History* (London: Fontana Books, 1966), p. 61.

acceptable to others, not because they are untrue (which they might be), but because they seem to lean upon what one reviewer called my "proper and proud Arminianism," an inheritance all but lost in one of the least theologically articulate of world confessions.

Traditional theological attitudes are not simply confessional. There is also the weight of what is generally taken to be "biblical theology," or even "kerygmatic theology," about which I shall say a good deal. Finally, there is the weight of the church's creeds, prayers, and liturgies. Here I may be content to quote some striking words of Karl Rahner:

If anyone were to attempt to discover the biblical foundation of scholastic Christology, he would reach the conclusion, which does not seem false or unjust, that it contrives to get along with a mere handful of texts from the Bible.[2]

But the same is true of Reformed Christology; or of what is often called "Catholic Christianity," or "the Christianity of the creeds." All these formulations depended more or less upon the placing of Christian truth within a particular cultural, ethnic, or scientific world view. None can be assumed to have survival value in a radically different world such as that in which we live today. The only question which remains is whether the formulations were, perhaps, perversions.

Necessarily, this means some attempt to discover an "essential" or "true" Christianity. There is no other path open to serious Christian thinking. Our argument is that the attempt has to be made in each age, with a good heart, without presuming that any age can see or say everything, or say it

[2] "Current Problems in Christology," *Theological Investigations* (London: Darton, Longman and Todd, 1961), I, 168.

for all ages. The survival of Jesus can only depend on a new assessment of Jesus. A new assessment of Jesus can only be made in the thought forms of each age. The thought forms of this age are "secular." Our claim is that this secular stance uncovers something new in the Jesus-story. Our claim is also that that "something new" is the essence, the truth, the kernel. One can but take courage that one, at least, of the warnings against such enterprises comes from one who for his day performed no less a task, von Harnack:

There is something touching in the anxiety which everyone has to rediscover himself, together with his own point of view and his own circle of interest, in this Jesus Christ, or at least to get a share in him.[3]

Unhappily and happily, there is no alternative.

---

[3] Adolf von Harnack, *What Is Christianity?* (New York: Harper Torchbooks, 1957), p. 3. Cf. E. L. Mascall's complaints against recent theologians who "tend to retain the word 'Christianity' while applying it to something that nobody would normally describe as Christianity, and then to say that this new thing is 'real Christianity,' or 'authentic Christianity,' or 'the essence of Christianity,' or 'what Christianity really is'" (*The Secularization of Christianity* [New York: Holt, Rinehart, and Winston, 1966], p. 6).

PART I

A Moment of Truth for Theology ?

Chapter 1

WHO IS CHRIST FOR MAN TODAY?

The question, "Who is Christ for man today?" is, of course, Dietrich Bonhoeffer's question. It can be taken in at least three senses.

The first sense is, who for man today is the Christ? That is, who corresponds to the "anointed one," in the sense that Jesus was the "anointed one" (*Messias, Christos*) for his generation? Who is for our day what Jesus was for his day? Who is the twentieth-century "anointed one"? Who is "God's new Messiah," as James Russell Lowell has it in his hymn "Once to every man and nation"? In this sense, all one needs to know from Jesus of Nazareth are the broad characteristics of what the Messiah, the anointed one of God, looks like. One then looks for someone other than him, who is to us now what he was to his generation.

The second sense in which one can take this question of Bonhoeffer's is almost identical, but distinguishable. Who for man today can be "Christ"? What *aspect* of man today

27

can be Christ? That is, what aspect of the human condition seems to correspond in our day to what Christ was in his day? What is Christ-existence, messianic-existence, for contemporary man? What kind of life can be "Christ-life" today? What kind of life can do for men today what Jesus did for yesterday? This question begins with modern life, asks what pattern of existence is most relevant or redemptive within it, and then asks: Can we find an embodiment of this around which we may build a faith for this day?

The third way of taking Bonhoeffer's question moves away from the strict sense of the German *wer*, but in Christian discussion becomes more feasible. It asks: What is the one Christ distinctively for this day? What is he like for *us*? What is Christ as our contemporary now? What aspect of the *totus Christus*, the whole Christ, the Christ in all his offices, is being manifest to us by Christ at this time?

I want mainly to take this third sense of the question, not ignoring the other two but insisting, indeed, that you come to the other two by trying to answer the third.

There are two questions pressing in on every sensitive Christian. One question is: Is the Jesus of the Gospels in any sense relevant to the search for a Christianity suited to a modern, "secular" age? This question tends to begin with the modern, secular situation and seek for parts of the story which can still fit in with it. It was in this mood that John Robinson wrote *Honest to God* and *The New Reformation?*. These books were not primarily even asking what the Gospels claimed about Jesus. Rather were they exercises in discovering what a "truly contemporary person" (whoever that could be) could do or believe or think which might be shown to have some relation with Christ.[1] This is, of course, a highly relevant procedure.

[1] J. A. T. Robinson, *Honest to God* (Philadelphia: The Westminster Press, 1963); *The New Reformation?* (The Westminster Press, 1965), esp. p. 52.

But there is another question which has to be given equal —or greater—weight within any Christian discussion. It relates to the basic core of Christianity itself. It asks, What actually is all this about Jesus? What is the Jesus-story really saying? What form of human existence is demanded by this whole Jesus-phenomenon which creates the New Testament? What does this Jesus-story say about man in his nonreligious existence, about man in society, about man in separation from God? Now, all these things apply as equally to twentieth as to first century man. Obviously, we shall approach the question through our own minds, just as those in the first century did, or those in the twelfth or fifteenth or nineteenth. Every theologian writes as he lives—as a child of his own age, anguishes, triumphs, prejudices, and insights. To this extent every age produces a Christ "after its own image"—or at least, as I would prefer to say, highlights those aspects of the one, whole Christ which speak most cogently to it.

The word "secular" probably describes the twentieth-century stance most simply. God has been edged out of the vast areas of knowledge, experience, culture, and science in which he was formerly included. God has ceased to be part of the intellectual or cultural "establishment." So that "our" Christ will inevitably "look" secular. What we have to discover is whether the Christ of the New Testament was secular, and if so, what kind of secularity was shown there.

Yet we need to be careful in our use of the word "secular" —a word which we will consider in more detail later. But let us at least immediately point out that the first century had no sense of God's nearness, or the nearness of spiritual things, which is denied to us. It was largely in the nineteenth century that the myths of "spiritual consciousness" emerged. The first century Jew knew no immediate consciousness of the spiritual any more than his Gentile contemporary. He was, in that sense, as "secular" as any modern man. That is, he lived in a world in which the only gods there were were very hidden and unknown indeed! (Cf. Acts 17:23.)

So that we come to our subject without any necessity for shame or self-consciousness, as if our "secular" stance put us out of accord with the Gospels. The God of the Bible had always been a hidden God, a God served by his people Israel in strictly practical ways of honesty and integrity. He was not "known" to them except in his deeds. The moments when an Israelite "saw the Lord . . . , high and lifted up" (Isa. 6:1) were very, very rare indeed.

Much contemporary theology seeks still to avoid the question, "Who is Christ for man today?" not because it does not at least intend to take "today" seriously, but because it does not wish to be left standing only by "Christ." It is initially too concerned with "relevance." It fears that Christ might be irrelevant. Perhaps the tragedy with Christian theology has been that it has not been serious enough and that it has taken itself too seriously. On the one hand, it has purported to deal with "the great issues of life and death," but in fact has appeared to most men—and many Christians—to be dealing only with peripheral matters. On the other hand, it has believed in itself and its own self-consistency more ardently and seriously than it has believed in the mysteries which, when pressed, it would confess to exist beyond it.

Christian theology's lack of seriousness appears particularly in what might be called its "evangelical doctrines." In principle and intention, the evangelical doctrines are the description of how a human being comes into contact with the ultimate reality of all things. "Justification by faith" was a classic way of stating that such a contact was both a divinely inspired, occurrence and also an utterly inexplicable human "leap." But in evangelical doctrine, this way of describing man's dealing with the ultimate is reduced to being part of the way in which the individual soul privately sorts himself out, "gets right with God," or "gets converted."

The great New Testament doctrines of the incarnation, death, and resurrection of Christ (the ministry is always omitted) are all reduced to this "point of contact" (*Anknüpfungspunkt*). The necessary prerequisite is a sense of sin, and the necessary prerequisite of that is sin! So the total work of Christ is understood as a "death for sins" which one "appropriates" by the act of decision or belief.

While almost the whole of evangelical theology, and almost all church practice, still works on some such scheme as this, the mounting witness of Christians is that this does not in any way correspond to their own experience. This negative point I have elaborated enough already in *Christ and Methodism* by suggesting that "Christ for man today" is primarily Lord, not Savior. Two further points may be added.

First, there is mounting evidence from Christian people not only that the so-called evangelical scheme does not apply to them, but that they are living lives of depth, significance, joy and acceptance, suffering and sacrifice, and it would be unthinkable that such lives would not in fact have anything to do with the Christ-events. There *is* a depth of otherness, of hidden acceptance, of "joy in sufferings," which the modern secular Christian has. The cross and resurrection do not seem to correspond to an experience of darkness and enlightenment (except as repeated and repeatable experiences, which is not what "conversion" has meant). But the incarnation does lead him to a radically different view of humanity, a Christian humanism. And the healing ministry does lead him to vocational commitment not merely where he can "express his personality," but where man's suffering is healed. And the cross does halt his will to desert the fight with the knowledge that suffering works endurance, and endurance produces character (Rom. 5:3). And the resurrection does give him in the midst of uncertainty and fear the unbounded possibility of God's acceptance of the life in Christ and its fullness beyond.

Thus the Christ-events, delivered from their straitjacket within the salvation-scheme, become life-giving for the Christian. Must not theology now follow experience?

But, second, is there not something more? Could the answer to the question, "How do I encounter Christ?" or "How do I encounter ultimate reality, or joy, or significance?" (and the Christian, of course, identifies the two) be found within life itself? Was the evangelical answer, "By the leap of faith," wrong not because it expected too much, but because it did not expect enough, and because it did not understand what "faith" means?

For does not any man, believing or atheist, *in fact and in reality* respond to the incarnation when by some deed he shows his corporate existence within the body of Christ, which is the deeds of Christ being done? The incarnation is proclaimed and entered into and ultimately encountered ("savingly" encountered?) when the modern world responds with humanity to its racial, cultural, and religious unity, and when a man gives his life in order that this may come to pass, that a "new man" may emerge. The ministry of Christ is proclaimed and entered into and encountered every time a young person chooses service above success in his choice of vocation. The cross is proclaimed and entered into and encountered when man endures for the sake of his brother. The resurrection dawns when the life in Christ is greeted with unexpected success!

And the church, of course, becomes Christian when these glorious mysteries, proclaimed in its liturgy and fought out in its fellowship, are bodied forth in actions for the world to see and to benefit by.

Must not theology now follow the living, total Christ?

The other tragedy, about the church's self-faith and self-consistency and about its lack of ultimate seriousness due to its taking itself too seriously, follows from this. When one reads the classic or even recent productions of our theological thinkers, it is hard really to believe that it is actually God, the creator and preserver of myriad universes and of all mankind, who is contained or even hinted at within the careful claims of evangelical theology, with its "for me," its "personal experience," its "confident assurance." Could it not be that the glorious mysteries of the faith have been personalized to death? That the whole truth about God's creation, which was what was being shown in Christ, *cannot* be crammed into a private soul? That the *milieu divin* is the whole creation, and we conscious or intended Christians just the slave boys of the universal design which breaks out wherever, hiddenly in the world or (we hope) openly in the church, the great mysteries of Christ are repeated? Can we not at least start to laugh at ourselves?

In the next two chapters I shall attempt to summarize the present situation in theology, at least in two areas. It will become plain that I cannot stand unequivocally in either group—either the British so-called "radicals" or the continental-American "secularizers."

All this may appear rather tedious to people who wish to have this theologian in as neat a package as those into which he bundles his older contemporaries in the next two chapters! So that we might as well set down at this stage that the question, "Who is Christ for man today?" can only be asked by any man in fear and trembling. Those who speak loudest are most conscious that they can but stand on the bit of ground that has been given them and try to help others, even, to see something also. But they do not ever think that

33

they are saying *everything,* or saying it *finally!* Yet they must, simply because the ground they stand on is not ultimately theirs, *sound* as if they can say everything, and finally!

Thus, in this volume, I have not bothered to quote when it merely appeared that another writer was saying the same thing that I wished to say. But I have sometimes gone out of my way to quote from writers who appear to be saying almost the same thing, but who say it with a difference of nuance which to me is both important and instructive. This is not perversity. It is the only way in which theological discussion can proceed. It means that a writer criticizes most those whom he most appreciates. I do not need to take issue at all with those who are fundamentally out of sympathy with what those called by others "New Theologians" are trying to do. So that "you always hurt the one you love" is peculiarly true for those who today man what Dr. Robinson has called the "radical boat."

At any rate, I have tried to retain two cardinal laws which might even be recommended to others.

First, that we do not misquote each other, that we retain a scrupulous regard for each other in the midst of disagreement. Martin Thornton got bouquets for his dictum about the New Theologians (his caps, by the way) being "as men writing wonderful cookery books, having first blown up the kitchen." [2] It invites retort, of course. Are the old theologians like cooks churning out the old stuff from the old kitchen while everyone else is eating downtown? Modern Christians are not articulate (they have had the old recipes pumped into them so long, they are now terrified to eat at all). They answer, though—with their feet.

Second, that we keep a sense of humor, because nobody can really see "the way things really are." Tillich confessed a

[2] *The Rock and the River* (New York: Morehouse-Barlow Co., 1965), p. 35.

"pervasive sense of joy, the joy of creative communion, of giving and taking." [3] Bonhoeffer talked of the "conviction, detachment and humour" in Barth's *hilaritas*: "a certain boldness and defiance of the world and of public opinion, a steadfast certainty that what one does benefits the world, even though it does not approve." [4] The theologian especially has to live by *pecca fortiter!* Desperately, we need the humor at ourselves which is boldness. I have tried to remember.

"What is Christ for man today?" means, then, first and foremost a search in a new way for the meaning of Christ, using the perspective of our time (for no other is available to us) but taking our leave immediately of Protestant theologies based on "experience," or "man today," as firmly as we would part company with Catholic or Protestant theologies of ontology or philosophy. We shall not be able to avoid these questions as we proceed. But most of this book is taken up with an examination of parts of the traditions about Jesus Christ which we have in the Gospels. This is due to the fact that I believe one of the main shortcomings with much recent theology has been that Jesus Christ has become a mere "cipher" by which other concepts—faith, history, being, or whatever—have been debated. It will appear how all this has produced a faulty picture of Christ. Perhaps I should end here, then, with a word about what I mean by this "Christocentricity."

Theology begins and ends only in Jesus Christ. This is not exclusive, but all-inclusive, as the New Testament claims. But the challenge of the Cambridge so-called radicals and the efforts of the sociologist-secularizers must be analyzed in the

---

[3] *Ultimate Concern: Tillich in Dialogue,* ed. D. Mackenzie Brown (New York: Harper & Row, 1965), p. xvi.

[4] Dietrich Bonhoeffer, *Letters and Papers from Prison* (New York: The Macmillan Company, 1962), p. 143.

light of Christ. I would dissent from many of the stances taken by Karl Barth, but I would stand by him when he writes about the church's attempts to go beyond Jesus Christ in the consideration and definition of God, and in speech about God:

When theology allows itself on any pretext to be jostled away from that name, God is inevitably crowded out by a hypostatised image of man. Theology must begin with Jesus Christ, and not with general principles, however better, or, at any rate, more relevant and illuminating, they may appear to be: as though He were a continuation of the knowledge and Word of God, and not its root and origin, not indeed the very Word of God itself. Theology must also end with Him, and not with supposedly self-evident general conclusions from what is particularly enclosed and disclosed in Him: as though the fruits could be shaken from this tree; as though in the things of God there were anything general which we could know and designate in addition to and even independently of this particular.[5]

Yet this does not mean, in any sense whatever, that we do not ask radical questions. Rather, it means that we remain in radical uncommitment until we see what radical questions come to us from the Gospels!

So that, at the end, we shall find ourselves even asking whether the "who" of Jesus does not overthrow even the many-sided Christology we have received. Too often the questions asked about Jesus have been "how?" and "what?" whereas the only legitimate questions are "who?" and "where?" "How did God become man in Jesus?" "How is Christ present in the church?" "How am I saved from my sins?" should be replaced by "Who is Jesus Christ?" "Who is present and contemporaneous with us here?" "Who is the one who is 'for me'?" "Where may I find him now?"

[5] Barth, *Church Dogmatics* (Edinburgh: T. & T. Clark, 1957) II/2, 4.

Chapter 2

THE CAMBRIDGE "RADICALS"

The fundamental theological questions have been set for our generation mainly by John Robinson and the others of the "Cambridge" or "South Bank" school. That is to say, the way we address questions regarding Christ tends to be the way John Robinson did. We shall therefore consider one or two of the most recent writings from theologians of this "school"; although in general they are not happy about being called a school.[1] For anyone not of their number, their common approach to theology marks them off as a quite definite element in the British theological scene—even if only because their approach is so typically English!

In *Religion and Humanism*, Howard Root has put forward the following alternatives as being answers to the question: What is the essential thing in Christianity? First,

[1] Cf. David L. Edwards, *The Honest to God Debate* (Philadelphia: The Westminster Press, 1963), pp. 20-44; and also Alan Richardson, *Religion in Contemporary Debate* (The Westminster Press, 1966).

he describes what he calls the position of the *objectivists*. This takes the Christian essence as "the original or traditional or objective substance of the gospel, asserting that God has acted in history, especially in Christ." Root himself prefers what he describes as the *subjectivists'* position: "Man's need for a way of life or integration of personality. The words and deeds of Jesus are the gospel, the good news, because they enable men to see themselves better and live better lives; the whole supernaturalistic framework is outmoded." [2]

So, from the beginning we have two possible answers to the question of what Christianity is about. The first is the traditionalist, the objectivist, deistic, if you like. Beginning there, you go straight into a discussion of the possibility of basing such an assertive position on history, on what has been revealed in history. The second, the subjectivist position, could be described, I suppose, as the humanistic, the "slippery slope which leads to subjectivism," as Root calls it.

Are there any other options? Alec Vidler, in one of his recent studies, put forward what he regards as a third possibility. He suggests that we "start from the admission that there is at present no one form of belief or unbelief that can be conclusively shown to be more reasonable or self-commending than all others." [3] I think this delightful position would be generally preferred by most of us! On this, at least we can agree that we disagree and at least we can agree that there is no one basis for making any progress! Yet, if this is "a third way of responding to the present theological situation," then it seems very like throwing in the towel, or at least sitting on the touchline to see how the game goes. Vidler, in pursuit of this third option, asks for "the elucidation of the options that are open to reasonable men in this age of the world." Well, in a sense we would all agree, but

[2] Root in *Religion and Humanism* (B.B.C. Publications, 1964), pp. 28-35.
[3] *Twentieth Century Defenders of the Faith* (New York: The Seabury Press, 1965), p. 118.

this still leaves wide open the question: Is there a Christian option? And this would lead on to the question: What if the Christian option cannot be shown to be more reasonable or self-commending? Do you then throw it away because you wish to be reasonable rather than Christian? Or is it a false dichotomy from the beginning to say that you either have to be reasonable or Christian, or that you have to begin exclusively with reason?

So therefore we are cast back upon the question: What is the Christian faith? And is it inseparable from one Jesus Christ? I would argue that you have to begin with this one Jesus Christ before you can come on to the question about contemporary possibility, contemporary reasonableness and contemporary self-commendation. And then you would have to go to the only place you can go to answer this question —the New Testament—and ask not simply what the words are saying, but what is being meant by them. And in the light of that, you could raise the question: What could be Christian existence for man today? How can man today involve himself in the self-understanding that is contained in the picture of Christian existence in the New Testament?

We are all men of our age and we cannot be anything else. So, therefore it is an important question: What can we do with the Christian faith so that modern man can take some notice of it? It is an important question for ourselves: What can we as modern men make of the Christian faith? But taken as simply as that, it always leads to a reduction of Christianity to what can be accepted by man at any particular moment. Cambridge theology has been doing this, I would guess, ever since the Enlightenment hit theology in the form of deism two hundred years ago.[4] By and large, the kind of

---

[4] We need a thorough history of doctrine which would do for English theology of the last 250 years whát the meticulous *Dogmengeschichtes* do for Continental theology. Many of T. F. Torrance's writings whet our appetite for it.

Cambridge theology represented by John Robinson or Alec Vidler or any other of its spokesmen is a more theological way of putting the question: In what way can we make modern man take any notice of God? And this immediately becomes the question: What kind of God can we think up that natural man will approve of or find easy to get along with? [5]

Now, this question about the contemporary acceptability of Christianity is a necessary one in anyone's mind at any time. Every Christian thinker must address questions to Christ in the thought-forms of his own day and in the social milieu and the psychological situation of his own day. But this is not to say, as Robinson says and basically as Tillich said before him, that we will allow modern man's questions to be heard and then will simply let these questions determine the shape of the Christianity we will find.

John Robinson himself is schizophrenic at this point—and perhaps speaks for so many precisely because he is. In *The New Reformation?* he asks for an "inductive faith"—a faith which begins "from the other end," not from Christian dogma but from man's experience in the world.[6] In this, of course, Robinson is simply following Tillich, as he freely admits. His passionate desire is to provide an open forum where every man can "see the meaning of his experience." At the same time, Robinson desires to take seriously what he calls "the centre." Jesus Christ, he thinks, discloses himself as the gracious neighbor first, and only then can be recognized as Master and Lord. The passages Robinson most frequently refers to are the parable of the sheep and the goats in Matthew 25 and the resurrection stories of the hidden Christ on the Emmaus Road (Luke 24) and beside the lake

[5] One recalls the recent collection, *The God I Want,* ed. James Mitchell (London: Constable & Co., 1966).

[6] *The New Reformation?* pp. 38-46.

(John 21). Indeed they are passages which, as he says, have "compelling power for our generation,"

for they all tell of one who comes unknown and uninvited into the human situation, disclosing himself as the gracious neighbor before he can be recognized as Master and Lord. And with these passages I would link the story of the Foot-washing in John 13, where, even to those who call him Lord and Master, he can make known the meaning of that lordship only by becoming the servant of all. Together they speak of a *way into* the truth as it is in Jesus which I believe has distinctive significance for our age. It is indeed central to the Christian revelation for any age. For the very meaning of the Incarnation is that the divine enters through the stable door of ordinary human history and everyday experience. It was only in man and as man that men could come to see the Son of God.[7]

This is a position with which I personally find myself in great sympathy. Yet one is bound to ask some questions about it. First, is this unknown and uninvited Christ the *only* Christ available to us? Second, what exactly is this Christ doing in the world? Do the Gospels have no more to tell us? Third, what kind of christological picture do we derive from the Gospels? (Too often Robinson thinks of doctrine or orthodoxy as a static block that you have to come to accept in the end!) Fourth, what kind of church and worship will feed man's understanding of this Christ? (Robinson here remains conservatively Anglican when it comes to putting the cards on the table.)

In my earlier book, *Christ and Methodism*, I outlined some of the answers of this present book in rather summary and dogmatic form. The Bishop of Woolwich gave the book a long, critical review entitled "Rocking the Radical Boat, Too." After insisting that "as Christian radicals we all have our own accents and idioms, and we must speak in them,"

[7] *Ibid.*, p. 36.

41

he goes on to criticize my position as "anti-humanistic Christocentric fundamentalism." He quotes a passage from *Christ and Methodism* as follows: "The 'experiential' line to certainty is now closed to us. Only One Authority remains: Jesus Christ. And what a mercy that is for men today! For only One Authority has been given: Jesus Christ!"

Then Robinson comments:

But this is fundamentalism, even if Christ is substituted for the Pope, or the Book, or the Inner Light, or the Methodist doctrine of Assurance. It ignores the fact that the answer to Bonhoeffer's question, "What (or who) is Christ for man today?" is extremely uncertain. One cannot simply start there as though it were mercifully provided as the knot in the thread.

Nor, when one does come to Christ at the centre (as, of course, one must), can he be presented in the exclusivist terms in which Dr. Vincent writes. It is just not true (for me at any rate) that "the only word of God we can know is his word in the cross" or "his Word made flesh and dwelling among us." Nor is the incarnation the cutting off by God of every "spiritual" approach to God or reality.

So far as Robinson is concerned, he confesses:

I would start unashamedly from a Christian humanism as broadly based as "all there is in human life" (to adapt the claim of the *News of the World*). I am convinced with Howard Root (in *Soundings*) that a recovery of natural theology is an urgent priority and that its starting point is "sharpened awareness." That is why I believe that the approach of Tillich with his "answering theology" is a necessary complement to that of Bonhoeffer. Indeed, I am inclined to think that my holding together of the two (for which I tend to be criticized with such incredulity especially by the disciples of Bonhoeffer) may be the only original contribution of *Honest to God*.[8]

Now, I have quoted Dr. Robinson's views in detail here

[8] Robinson in *Prism*, March, 1965, pp. 6-10, 78.

because, being written in response to my own, they pinpoint the areas which are already delineated between us. I am not sure that either of us would want to be held to every word! With regard to Dr. Robinson's accusation of "anti-humanistic Christocentric fundamentalism," I have already pointed out that "positivism" would have been a more correct term, as I am certainly no fundamentalist! Perhaps I may be allowed to quote part of my reply.

But "anti-humanistic Christocentric" does not bother me so much. If by "anti-humanistic" is meant that I am not prepared simply to take the contemporary world and pretend that the Kingdom will come if we can only use "the good in it," then I am anti-humanistic and so is the New Testament. If by "Christocentric" is meant that I believe that there can be no genuine discovery of "Christ for man today" which does not take the basic Christological categories of the New Testament seriously, then I am Christocentric. (And if this is "fundamentalism," then I am fundamentalist!) For the present debate is simply going to cease to be a *Christian* debate, unless the essential Christian, that is Christological, categories are retained. What the Christian categories *mean* is absolutely open. My book is but one modest stab at an answer. But unless we begin with the Christian categories, and how modern man can be "in Christ," then we are worshipping secularism and not Christ.

Put like this, I may appear conservative and obscurantist. In fact, I would claim that my position is far more radical than Dr. Robinson's, as it takes the essential radicalism of Christ and throws the contemporary Church up against it. Dr. Robinson's radicalism tends to take the contemporary world and throw the Church up against that. We need both confrontations. Perhaps, to do one is already to do the other. Is there, to trot for a minute behind Barth's "humanity of God," a Secular Christ, a Christ who already speaks through the secular? Dr. Robinson would agree, I think, that there is. All I wish to do is to put some work in at the Christological end, at least till he has time to do the New Testament study on

Christology he is longing to get to! Meantime, we stick to Matthew 25 and Colossians 1 (cf. *The New Reformation?* p. 36).[9]

Cambridge "radicalism," then, is humanism, not Christianity. Meantime, Robinson's American authorities have come to occupy a position which is both too tentative and too atheistic really to serve as undergirding for the essentially and typically English moderation of Cambridge liberalism. William Hamilton, whose earlier book, *The New Essence of Christianity*,[10] earned Robinson's praise, now declares that we can only proclaim a truly radical Christianity if we proclaim "the death of God," not simply as a recognition of his absence, but as a dogmatic statement of his nonexistence.[11] The "theologian" of today really doesn't believe in God, whatever that means, or that there is *a* God, or that God *exists*.[12] Hamilton would agree—as I would—with Thomas Altizer that the theologian's first duty is to Christ.[13] Many of the things which Hamilton and Altizer have to say about Christ, although often fragmentary and unsystematic, are, at least to my mind, full of possibilities. How I stand in relation to the "death of God" position will emerge in chapter 14. My point at the moment is that our critique of Cambridge "radicalism" as being not truly radical finds an echo now from those who seek what they describe as a "radical theology" of "Christian atheism."

Whether we can claim the term "radical" for a "radical Christocentricity" remains to be seen.

[9] *Prism,* June, 1965, pp. 31-34. I am referring to the "questions relating to the person and work of Christ" which he would like to follow up "when time allows" (*The Honest to God Debate,* p. 266).

[10] (New York: Association Press, 1961).

[11] Thomas J. J. Altizer and William Hamilton, *Radical Theology and the Death of God* (Indianapolis: Bobbs-Merrill, 1966).

[12] Hamilton, "Thursday's Child," in *Radical Theology,* p. 88.

[13] Altizer, *The Gospel of Christian Atheism* (Philadelphia: The Westminster Press, 1966), p. 10.

Chapter 3

THE SECULAR THEOLOGIANS

The word "secular" is as elusive as it is fascinating in contemporary discussion. I shall take it to mean "that which is separated from any metaphysical reference," "that which pertains to this present physical world."

I want to use "secular" in this simple sense, without wishing to comment too much on the question whether or not we are living in a peculiarly secular age today, though assuming for the argument that man is basically secular. "Secularization," that is, the process whereby post-Renaissance man has more and more come to run his world without any exterior reference, has been claimed as a fruit of Christianity. A. Th. van Leeuwen argues that the beginnings of the process of secularization are to be found in the religion of Israel:

Where the Gospel is believed, there is the truth accepted that there can be no returning to the age of "religion." This demolishing of the mediaeval *Corpus Christianum* represents—as it also anticipates—the doing away with every *corpus religiosum*, just as the destruction of the Temple at Jerusalem signifies that all our temples are, in principle, abolished.[1]

Or, similarly, Albert van den Heuvel:

It is within Israel that the sacred kingship is destroyed, the holy temple brought down, and the holy people scattered among the nations. In the New Testament, this history reaches its climax at the cross of Golgotha where God's judgment is passed upon the Messiah of Israel, upon God's own appointed Son.[2]

Cornelius van Peursen believes that the biblical story belongs, not to myth or to ontology, but to *functional* ways of thought:

In the period of myth, the main issue was *that* something is; in the period of ontological thinking, it was *what* something is; in the period of functional thinking, it is *how* something is, how it functions.[3]

The Jew meant by "truth" that which *worked*, which could be depended upon. Thus was God known only in his deeds.

Van Leeuwen, van den Heuvel, van Peursen, and the other writers in this field have so far had surprisingly little to say about the Jesus of the Synoptic Gospels.[4] I hope to

---

[1] *Christianity in World History* (New York: Charles Scribner's Sons, 1966), p. 409.

[2] "Secularisation as Freedom and Yoke," *Study Encounter*, I (1965), 59. This is a very useful review of much literature on the secularization discussion. Even better now is Coenraad van Ouwerkerk, "Secularism and Christian Ethics: Some Types and Symptoms," *Concilium*, V (May, 1967), 47-67.

[3] "Man and Reality: The History of Human Thought," *The Student World*, LVI (1963), 17.

[4] One might especially expect more from Gerhard Ebeling. Cf. his *Nature of Faith* (Philadelphia: Fortress Press, 1962). Arnold E. Loen, in *Secularization: Science Without God?* (London: SCM Press, 1967) does not really tackle the issues here being raised, and ignores the Gospels.

show that there is a great deal of fuel for the discussion, not all of it plain or unequivocal, in the Synoptic picture of Jesus. The work of Harvey Cox explicitly deals with this material, but we will postpone consideration of his analysis until we have studied the Synoptic material itself.

Dietrich Bonhoeffer described secularization as the "abandonment of a false conception of God, and a clearing of the decks for the God of the Bible." [5] By this, Bonhoeffer did not mean a "reduction" of the faith, but rather taking the faith in its wholeness seriously.

What do we mean by "God"? Not in the first place an abstract belief in his omnipotence, etc. That is not a genuine experience of God, but a partial extension of the world. Encounter with Jesus Christ, implying a complete orientation of human being in the experience of Jesus as one whose only concern is for others. This concern of Jesus for others the experience of transcendence. This freedom from self, maintained to the point of death, the sole ground of his omnipotence, omniscience and ubiquity. Faith is participation in this Being of Jesus (incarnation, cross and resurrection).[6]

Bonhoeffer's writings are fragmentary, and it is notoriously easy for all kinds of theologians to claim their descendance from him. He has become particularly the prophet for the secularizers. Yet, without wishing to claim Bonhoeffer's imprimatur for yet another theological "line," my own conviction remains that Bonhoeffer's vision of a nonreligious way of speaking about God, geared to "man come of age," was for him not simply an argument based on history and on the modern situation of man without God. Above all, this vision was determined by Bonhoeffer's picture of Christ —a picture which was of what I would call a "Secular Christ." I believe this vision of Christ as the New Man was

[5] *Letters and Papers from Prison*, p. 220.
[6] *Ibid.*, p. 237.

ultimately more determinative for his theology, even at the latter stages (when inconsistencies abound) than any picture of contemporary man in whose image a new form of Christ was to be created. I suggest that a new form of Christ is indeed demanded by our age—but it must be part of the one and only Christ of the New Testament. Within that total many-sided portrait are Christs enough for any age.

The questions which we must raise to the secularizers—assuming for a moment that they can be put together as a group—are fourfold.

First, is it the essence or stuff of Christianity which these writers believe themselves to be giving us, or is it merely an adaptation, be it modification or elaboration, of Christianity for this present age? The writings of the secularizers are obviously ambivalent at this point. Here they seem to be hand in hand with the more "liberal" of the Cambridge writings. They begin from the obviously good effort (which I believe is correct) to show that modern secular culture can and should be given a positive assessment by the Christian. Yet this laudable objective does not of itself contribute necessarily to a revelation of Christian truth, however much it may be a laudable and necessary contribution to evangelism in a secular world. Indeed, it is not hard for critics to show that this very praiseworthy effort lands the authors in somewhat ludicrous situations. This has been particularly true of Harvey Cox's excursions into work, sex, the university, etc.

Second, do the secularizers derive their essential and distinctive insights in any way from Jesus Christ? Most frequently they trace the origins of secularization to creation, the Exodus, the Sinai covenant (Harvey Cox), or to Hebrew religion as a whole (van Leeuwen). Van Leeuwen, of course, does trace the move toward an *oikoumene* to the preaching of the gospel to the Gentiles. Yet the possibility of a newness of the secular, given in Christ, does not come out clearly in these writings. Probably this has been due to their unquestioningly taking over the preconceptions of the biblical theology which was in vogue when these scholars were receiving their theological education—preconceptions based on an assumed or argued unity of the Bible, in which certain "lines" become clear which can then be shown to have persisted through Christian history.[7] At any rate, from the point of view of the New Testament or the Gospels, the secularizers have not so far appeared to take seriously the question of the ultimate or real nature of Christianity, or of the ultimate nature of the Christ—questions posed by the New Testament, and questions certainly not to be answered by a mere summary statement of what is said there, but only by the elucidation of the picture there presented in all its singularity.

The third question arises from the others but is distinguishable from them. The secularizers seem at times to be more than healthily under the dictates of one form or another of contemporary philosophy—another perversion from which Bonhoeffer has tried to secure our freedom. With van Buren it is Braithwaite and linguistic analysis; with Harvey Cox it is revised American personalism; with Gregor Smith it is Gogarten and Bultmann; with van Leeuwen, a basically Hegelian philosophy of history. Now, no theologian is so naïve as to believe that he can pursue serious theological inquiry without any sort of philosophical presupposition. But when the "form of Christ" which emerges in a theology is *determined* by some particular philosophical mood or theory, then what is given to "man today" ceases to be Christ.

The fourth question is this: Would the secularizers have the view they adumbrate of the Christian contribution to history if western culture had not, in fact, moved in the historical direction in which it has moved? One is reminded

[7] Cf. the scholars quoted in the next chapter.

of T. S. Eliot's *Idea of a Christian Society*,[8] based essentially upon a medieval situation of church and state. But one would have to raise with Denis Munby's notable reply[9] the question whether the abolition of all forms or establishments is a necessary "fruit of Christ's work" or whether this is only a comparable attempt to give Christ some place in the way history has actually gone in the western world. Van Leeuwen, not dissimilarly, raises the question whether the movement from the old autocratic society to the new technocratic secular society is a *necessary* fruit of the gospel, in the same way as the "rise of capitalism" was of a post-Medieval Christendom.[10] Cox imagines the goal of an open community of free, mature persons as the goal revealed in Christ; yet *historically* this is difficult to demonstrate when freedom has so often been secured by anti-Christian or non-Christian forces, while the goal itself seems indistinguishable from secular, humanistic goals of the present century.

These questions are intended as questions, and not as criticisms, much less exposées. In raising them one is necessarily less than just to each writer in specific instances. Yet, since the extent and the depth of Christian thinking in this area will undoubtedly and rightly be carried further, it is important, it seems to me, to step back a little and survey the methodology and results of the secularizers. These writers are not thoughtless optimists. As van Leeuwen says: "As the seeds grow, so the seeds of Satan grow among the rest. The kingdom of Christ and the kingdom of antichrist both have the ends of the earth and all the nations as their final goal." [11]

[8] *The Idea of a Christian Society* (New York: Harcourt, Brace & World, 1940).

[9] D. L. Munby, *The Idea of a Secular Society* (New York: Oxford University Press, 1963).

[10] So R. H. Tawney, *Religion and the Rise of Capitalism* (Holland Lectures, 1922).

[11] *Christianity in World History*, p. 407.

So far, the only criticism of the secularizers has come from a rather conservative standpoint. Most recently, J. E. L. Newbigin has argued as follows:

Firstly, the secular society is conceivable only if religion continues to be a living reality. Secularity is not by itself enough to sustain by itself a human society in being.

Secondly, the idea of a secular society can only be rightly understood in the context of a biblical understanding of history.[12]

With all respect, I cannot see that these points take up the debate at any deeply Christian level. The first does not raise the question about Christ, in whose name the attack on religion has been made. The second already concedes the notion of a historical development toward secularization which is sufficiently apparent from many secularizers. Newbigin points out the dangers of optimism, but that has already been pointed out by the writers themselves.

Now, the argument of the present volume is not an attempt to redirect the total effort in this area; this would be beyond the power of any writer. It is, however, to argue that there is an essential secularity of the gospel, an essential secularity of Christ; but that this secularity itself must be allowed to determine the view the modern Christian takes of his world, and, more importantly, the place the modern Christian understands himself to be occupying within that world.

With this I cannot but link the rediscovery which I see beginning to take place in Bonhoeffer's writings of a Christ stripped of the perversions of religion, of philosophy, of ecclesiology. The Christ who has been perverted by these things is not the Christ of the New Testament. The Christ of the New Testament is discovered in his essential secularity.

[12] *Honest Religion for Secular Man* (Philadelphia: The Westminster Press, 1966), pp. 134 ff.

Eberhard Bethge has thus summarized some of Bonhoeffer's hints into this area:

But who is Jesus? . . . He is the man for others against individualistic inwardness. He is the lonely and forsaken without transcendent escape. He worships not in provinciality but in the midst of real life. He, though longing for him, does not experience the *deus ex machina*. Thus, the time for religion might have gone, but not the time for Jesus.[13]

Let us summarize our argument so far. The point I am seeking to make is not that what Cambridge or the secularizers make of Christ is wrong. On many points we shall find them true and faithful. It is rather, first, that they do not take seriously the Gospel picture of Jesus. And second, it is that the points at which they become radical, significant, or relevant are the points at which these theologians do not seem to depend explicitly on the "one word" of God to man in Jesus Christ.

What that "one word" is all about is wide open. But it can only be discovered by what Oscar Cullmann has called "obedient listening to the strangeness of the Bible." Before we "obediently listen," however, we need to set our attempts within the context of contemporary study of the Gospels, and that we shall do in the next chapter.

---

[13] "Bonhoeffer," *Chicago Theological Seminary Register*, I (1961), 33; also now in *World Come of Age*, ed. R. Gregor Smith (Philadelphia: Fortress Press, 1967), pp. 22-88. On Bonhoeffer here, cf. now John A. Phillips, *Christ for Us in the Theology of Dietrich Bonhoeffer* (New York: Harper & Row, 1967).

Chapter 4

THE BIBLICAL THEOLOGIANS

The claim of this book is that the Gospel record of Jesus has a great deal that is salutary and surprising to say to the contemporary theological scene. In order that the record may be heard, however, we must set the scene in the field of biblical theology, and especially indicate what answers have come from this area in recent years and why the answers we may discover have not so far emerged.

Form criticism, pioneered by Rudolf Bultmann and others in the 1920's, directed attention to the church which wrote our Gospels and to the traditions within the oral period between the events and the time of writing.[1] The stories of the earthly words and deeds of Jesus are derived from a community which believed in him as risen Lord, coming son of man, and future judge. Moreover, the stories themselves as

[1] Cf. Hugh Anderson, *Jesus and Christian Origins* (New York: Oxford University Press, 1964). For an excellent survey of recent Gospel scholarship, a more popular work is Heinz Zahrnt, *The Historical Jesus* (New York: Harper & Row, 1963).

they were handed on or written down were influenced by the changing demands of the church's preaching, apologetic, and discipline.

Accordingly, it might be expected that "the meaning of it all," what the Gospels say about discipleship, etc., would have been of special interest. In what way did being a disciple mean something different in A.D. 70 from what it meant in A.D. 30 or 50? In what ways did the church's self-understanding differ from her Lord's intention? What relation did the words of Jesus inviting men to discipleship play in the kerygma of the church? Are there circumstances in the later life of the church which might have modified or exaggerated the claims of Jesus on his followers? Did the church's conception of Jesus himself move away from that which he taught his first disciples to have of him? Did the fundamental aim of Jesus—assuming we may get to it—become altered as the gospel became clothed in Jewish and Hellenistic salvation terms?

Surprisingly, many of these questions have not received the attention which might have been expected. This may well be due to the concentration of much Synoptic scholarship over the past forty years upon eschatology and messiahship. Indeed, within postwar biblical theology, the child of dialectical theology and form criticism, many elements in the Synoptic tradition seem to be quite "beyond the pale." This has not been due solely to deliberate neglect. Rather, it has been due to a concentration of energies in other directions that have become the accepted concerns of biblical theology.[2] The result has been a fairly general consensus which can be characterized as follows:

(1) The concern for the unity of the Bible, leading to a preference for reading the Synoptics in the light of the Bible

---

[2] A recent exception is the thoroughgoing study of W. D. Davies, *The Setting of the Sermon on the Mount* (New York: Cambridge University Press, 1964).

as a whole, more particularly in the light of Paul or Acts.

(2) The suspicion of the "Jesus of history" as over against the "Christ of faith," and the belief that only the latter is relevant to Christianity today.

(3) The belief that "the gospel" dates only from the resurrection and is characterized by the gift of faith, particularly in the atoning death on the cross.

(4) The fear that the words of Jesus have been so influenced by subsequent church situations as to be of little value as reliable records.

(5) The consequent preoccupation with the kerygma, the preaching of the early church.

If this is a correct analysis of the present situation, a criticism of these assumptions should do something to justify a more constructive view. We shall reserve No. 5 for chapter 11. It is largely the product of the other attitudes, as will become clear.

(1) *The concern of biblical theology with the unity of the Scriptures* is a natural reaction against the delight in contradictions seen in some older critical scholars. But there are dangers in this concern for unity. If one comes to the New Testament, for example, with a "doctrine" of the people of God, of election, or of the covenant derived from a systematic theology of the Old Testament, there is a very strong probability that what one finds there will fit in with these doctrines. But will one find what the New Testament is striving to say? What if God's new deed overturns as well as fulfills the old? A similar but more far-reaching criticism could be made against the tendency to describe New Testament theology in terms of specific words or terms rather than the distinctively Christian intention in using them, which, additionally, varies from writer to writer, and from occasion to occasion. The slavish employment of the massive

Theologisches Wörterbuch sometimes justifies such criticism.[3] Again, within the New Testament, many recent theologians have stressed the unity of the different "varieties of religion." But what if the variety is the work of the Holy Spirit? The "essential thing" is not so easily put into a slogan, because it neither was nor is a static thing, but relates to the continuing deed of God in Christ and the unfolding mystery of the life of men with their Lord.[4]

This unfolding mystery and continuing deed is precisely the theme of the Synoptic Gospels. But there cannot be any fruitful theological development of any of the elements within the Synoptic tradition unless the legitimacy is recognized of taking seriously the singular and often disconnected words and events relating to such an element; and that initially only with regard to what the words mean, and then only secondarily to what they must be held to mean in the light of other concepts. There is *Heilsgeschichte* in the Synoptics: but one must not begin with a Pauline conception of *Heilsgeschichte* and then judge the Synoptic one by it. One must (as Schweitzer urged!) take the words as they stand.

Moreover, this is not a one-sided affair. Once the value of the continuing relation of men with Christ on the pattern of that of the first disciples is recognized, many other elements outside the Synoptics suddenly take on greater significance. A new "unity" emerges: it is not a static unity, but one which stems from the actual life and work of the early church. It may well be questioned whether the popular "thoroughgoing kerygmatism" based on Acts provides in itself a more reasonable or more useful vantage point.

(2) *The dichotomy between the "Jesus of history" and the "Christ of faith"* was furthered by the advance of form

[3] Cf. James Barr, *The Semantics of Biblical Language* (New York: Oxford University Press, 1961), pp. 206-62.

[4] B. Reicke, "Einheitlichkeit oder verschiedene 'Lehrbegriffe' in der neutestamentlichen Theologie?" *Theologische Zeitschrift,* IX (1953), 401-15.

critical methods. It has been one of the factors which has caused the revived interest in Pauline and Reformation theology. But it has also led to a radical oversimplification of the content of the Synoptic Gospels. Despite refinements, this has been the outcome of the work of such writers as Anton Fridrichsen, who tended to make Christ so much the property of the church as to deny his priority before and superiority over it and also his independent existence apart from the church's preaching, dogma, and cult; Rudolf Bultmann, for whom the "historical" Jesus has value neither as event nor for theology; and John Knox, whose "Jesus of the community of believers" alone is of importance, and for whom, therefore, questions of Synoptic exegesis are of secondary importance since "faith" is without obligation to them.[5] The dichotomy continues in the present discussions of New Testament theologians on the continent.[6]

We shall have to return to this question a number of times. But I may make a few general comments here.

The dichotomy ignores the purely historical links between the pre-crucifixion disciples and the post-resurrection believers. Believing on quite false grounds that the Synoptics are without value for a doctrine of the Christian life, the modern interpreter has fallen back on the fideism of the other writings. But, as we shall see, faith for the twelve disciples continued to mean in the days of the church what it had meant in the days of his flesh—a committal of one's life, possessions, and future in trust and obedience to the Master. It did not mean a "decision" ("existential" or otherwise) with regard to certain theological or soteriological

[5] Cf. esp. John Knox, *The Death of Christ* (Nashville: Abingdon Press, 1958).

[6] Cf. the volume *Der historische Jesus und der kerygmatische Christus,* ed. H. Ristow and K. Matthiae (Berlin: Evangelische Verlagsanstalt, 1960). Cf. also *The Historical Jesus and the Kerygmatic Christ,* ed. C. E. Braaten and R. A. Harrisville (Nashville: Abingdon Press, 1964).

propositions. It meant a response to the life which was being manifest in Christ—either the life and destiny of Jesus in person or else the life and destiny of his body, the church.

Again, as we shall see, it is wrong to separate the "faith" of the church as if it had nothing to do with action; just as it is wrong to assume that the action of the disciples in the Gospels had nothing to do with faith. In the early church, as in Jesus' lifetime, we may imagine that the discovery of him as "Lord" was mixed up in, and sometimes even secondary to, "doing the things he said." There was, as Minear has put it, no exact discrimination "between the confessions of the first disciples and those of a subsequent generation," so that "the Passion story had the power to demonstrate the solidarity of all men in the sin of the original disciples." [7] "Faith" belonged as much to the pre-resurrection experiences as to the post-resurrection ones. It was "the Jesus of history" to whom response was made in both cases. And, we may conclude, by "Jesus of history" we do not mean a chronological recital of the saving facts of his life (such as a "kerygmatic" life of Jesus would alone give us), but the total impact of his person, ministry, teaching, miracles, and passion as constituting the first group of disciples and their successors in the church.

(3) *But is there gospel in this pre-resurrection Christ?* If the gospel consists in all that God did in and through Jesus Christ, then there can be no gospel without him. It cannot be a matter of indifference to the content of the Christian revelation that God has been traditionally assumed to have occupied himself for three years with the life of the man Jesus. Moreover, the "kerygmatic theological docetism" [8]

[7] Paul S. Minear, *The Kingdom and the Power* (Philadelphia: The Westminster Press, 1950), pp. 80-81.

[8] N. A. Dahl, "Der historische Jesus als geschichtswissenschaftliches und theologisches Problem," in *Kerygma und Dogma,* I (1955), 102-32. Cf. also A. N. Wilder, *Otherworldliness and the New Testament* (New York: Harper & Row, 1954), ch. 3.

of ignoring the pre-resurrection Christ results in a denuded gospel. The absence of social ethics or social concern in much recent theology may stem directly from this challenge to the wholeness of the picture of Christ which has come down to us. Where it is asserted that the one around whom our faith centers was not with us redeemingly "in the flesh," but only "in the spirit" and "through faith," then the church's retreat into "religion" is only to be expected.

The theology of discipleship should do something to correct this escapism. Salvation is involved in the whole life of Jesus, and in the whole life of everyone who comes into contact with him. The cross and resurrection are not events in comparison with which the previous work of Jesus is unimportant prelude. Rather are they the key to understanding the earthly ministry, preaching, and call to discipleship. The cross and resurrection for the disciple are not simply the object or subject of his faith, but are the content and meaning of his life, his following, his "works."

Beyond this we cannot go at the moment. Our whole thesis, however, will be that the Synoptic Gospels do indeed contain a message which is "gospel" or "good news" for man in comparison with which the "gospels" of Paul or Acts are complementary but secondary.

(4) *The fear that the Gospels do not contain reliable history* is not a new fear. It emerged as soon as the methods of historical criticism began to be used for the study of the Gospels over a century ago. The fear has taken on a new lease of life as a result of form criticism. Yet developments in the last ten years have not been unfruitful in this area. The question of the historicity of the Gospel narratives has been reopened from a number of points of view, and this has tended to break down the old historical/nonhistorical dichotomy as applied to the narratives.

(i) A number of the post-Bultmann scholars in Germany

have undertaken what has been described as a "new quest of the historical Jesus," which attempts to avoid the oversimplification and overoptimism of the liberal search for the Jesus of history and which concentrates on the "profound intentions, stances, and concepts of existence held by persons in the past, as the well-springs of their outward actions." [9] This view of history combines R. G. Collingwood with Martin Heidegger and, naturally, sees in the kerygma the essential issue of faith. The "lives" of Jesus in the Gospels are not relevant, and one must seek now to write a "kerygmatic life of Jesus." In fact, however, Ernst Fuchs, Ernst Käsemann, Günther Bornkamm, and others have not been content with debating this purely in terms of a "biography of Jesus" and in a number of studies have unquestionably opened the possibility that the Gospels themselves present a distinctive form of kerygma-in-historical-happenings in the deeds and words of Jesus.[10] Indeed, the new discoveries of Qumran and Nag Hammadi and the constant study of Gospel questions in the light of their Jewish background also give the lie to Bultmann's excessive historical skepticism.

(ii) Another group of scholars has asserted that "history is revelation"—that is, that rightly to understand history or to take it as it stands is to expose oneself to revelation. This position is taken, more or less, by scholars who otherwise stand in the widest possible divergence. Oscar Cullmann seeks to assert the completely historical nature of the Christian revelation over against the Bultmann and post-Bultmann schools, and stresses the impossibility of separating the biblical history from its Christian interpretation.[11] Carl Michal-

[9] J. M. Robinson, *The New Quest of the Historical Jesus* (Naperville, Ill.: Alec R. Allenson, 1959), p. 39.

[10] Ernst Fuchs, *Studies of the Historical Jesus* (Naperville, Ill.: Alec R. Allenson, 1964); Ernst Käsemann, *Essays on New Testament Themes* (Alec R. Allenson, 1964).

[11] Cullmann, *Salvation as History* (New York: Harper & Row, 1967), pp. 55 ff.

son, as a philosophical theologian much influenced by existentialism, yet argues for the place of Christianity essentially within history rather than philosophy or religion.[12] Wolfhart Pannenberg and others argue that revelation is mediated through historical events, and not only through Christ (Barth) or only through the kerygma and the individual's response to it (Bultmann); and that the historical-critical method confirms that revelation always comes mediately through the events of history.[13]

(iii) English writers, in the main, have approached the problem with their characteristic philosophically oriented viewpoint. Thus, T. A. Roberts argues[14] that historical discoveries can never of themselves provide conclusive proof. To prove that something happened does not prove, in any case, that it was a divine revelation. We cannot prove that the Gospel events and miracles did not happen; but we are in difficulties in knowing how we are to describe them—difficulties which are logical and philosophical.[15] Statements about the supernatural cannot be logically the same as empirical statements.

There is much else that could be said. When Martin Kähler launched his astounding essay on "the so-called historical Jesus and the biblical Christ" in 1898,[16] what he had in view was not the Jesus who lived in history, but rather the Jesus which the rational historical-critical methods sought to create. The latter Jesus was unobtainable! But there was

[12] Michalson, *The Rationality of Faith* (New York: Charles Scribner's Sons, 1963).

[13] *Theology as History,* ed. J. M. Robinson and J. B. Cobb (New York: Harper & Row, 1967), esp. pp. 221-76 by Pannenberg.

[14] *History and Christian Apologetic* (Naperville, Ill.: Alec R. Allenson, 1960).

[15] Roberts, "Gospel Historicity: Some Philosophical Observations," *Religious Studies,* April, 1966, pp. 185-202. Cf. the works of D. E. Nineham and H. E. W. Turner there cited.

[16] *Der sogenannte historischs Jesus und der geschichtliche biblische Christus* (Berlin, reprinted 1961).

a "real Jesus" who became the Christ of the church's faith. It is this Jesus of history who rose again who thus became the Christ of faith. As Cullmann has put it:

Since the *kerygma* has the historical Jesus as its object, some continuity must exist between the historical Jesus and the Christ of the *kerygma*. . . . The historical Jesus continues his work in the historic Christ, and hence only in this Christ of faith do we encounter the historical Jesus—not in a "life of Jesus" of modern scholarship.[17]

Here there may be a meeting between the *Heilsgeschichte* of Cullmann and the new historicism of Bultmann's followers. For "to seek history in the kerygma [as the post-Bultmann scholars attempt] means to seek the historical Jesus," even if this is not done for the purpose of reconstructing a life of Jesus but to establish the continuity between the proclamation made *by* Jesus and the proclamation made *of* Jesus, and thus the identity of the earthly Jesus and the exalted Christ.[18] James M. Robinson now sees between the kerygma and the historical Jesus "a very complicated relationship, which cannot be divided." [19] One recent scholar, Willi Marxsen, even reverses the argument of his teacher, Rudolf Bultmann, and argues that the kerygma is important because it points to the importance of the traditions about the earthly Jesus. The "what" and the "how" are the decisive questions about the whole matter, not the bare "that" it happened. We must test the Christ-kerygma by the Jesus-kerygma, for "the Jesus-kerygma gives the Christ-kerygma its content." [20]

[17] *Salvation as History*, p. 49.

[18] Heinz Zahrnt, *The Historical Jesus*, p. 146.

[19] "Kerygma and History in the New Testament" in *The Bible in Modern Scholarship*, ed. J. P. Hyatt (Nashville: Abingdon Press, 1965); *Zeitschrift für Theologie und Kirche* LXV (1965), 294-337.

[20] "Zur Frage nach dem historischen Jesus," *Zeitschrift für Theologie und Kirche*, LXII (1962), 575-80.

All this must lead inevitably and properly to a reopening of the Synoptic Gospels. This time, however, the presupposition will try to avoid either the extreme of liberalism, which presumes to tell a purely human story based on historical documents, or the extreme of form criticism, which concentrates merely upon the uses to which the early church in this or that situation might have been able to put this or that piece of the tradition. The presupposition now is that there is a Jesus who is the preached Jesus of the early church, who is at once the Lord presently reigning, and also the self-same Jesus who lived and died; and that the writers of the Gospels would in the main be concerned to show how the traditions about the earthly Jesus which they had received were in fact exactly the things which the believers in A.D. 65 or 70 needed to hear. If they could point out the immediate relevance of the piece of tradition, they would do so—hence, no doubt, many of the curious introductions and conclusions to pericopes. But there were also many things that simply had to be left as mysteries; and these were left. Thus, our approach is not "fundamentalist." But it might be called "skeptical" regarding the claims to be able to go behind the theological purpose of the writers (to say that the earthly Jesus now acted still) to sort out history from comment at every point.[21] Not only do we not have the equipment to do this; we do not *need* to do this.

[21] A spirited attack on the form critical method is to be found in the essays, *Vindications*, ed. Anthony Hanson (New York: Morehouse-Barlow Co., 1966), which deserves careful study, even if the approach is polemical. Cf. also C. F. D. Moule, *The Phenomenon of the New Testament* (London: SCM Press, 1967).

PART II

Mysterium Christi

E

Chapter 5

THE STRANGENESS OF JESUS

If one has not been struck before with the peculiarity of Jesus and the even stranger peculiarity, by contrast, of our Western picture of him, then a fortnight in Israel and Jordan, doing the Christian pilgrimage to the Holy Land, can be recommended.

It is not simply that the Western pilgrim (Protestant or Catholic) is disappointed. He has probably been warned about that. Rather it is to him "another world." In Jordan, he is in a Mohammedan, nomadic, Arab country, whose almost sole industry is Christian tourism. When he goes up to the Holy City, he is shown not only the place where Jesus ascended into heaven, but also where Mohammed did the same. He is shown not only the wailing wall, where no Jew wailed from 1947 to 1967, but also the site of Solomon's Temple and Herod's—except that the site is now covered by the great Mohammedan Dome of the Mosque. And when he goes to visit the places of the passion, he finds tiny Christian monastic communities guarding questionable sites locked behind enormous doors.

When he crosses the Mandelbaum Gate into "New Jerusalem," he finds himself in a vast, expansionist, Western, "secular" city, where what there is of Judaism that survives is mainly very contemporary, where the kibbutzim are not so much experiments in modern communism as carefully planned economic units geared to the creation of a "new" Israel. Humble Nazareth, the backwoods hamlet whose name was a standing joke in first-century Palestine (like Oswaldtwistle or Ramsbottom: "Can any good come out of—?"), is now a thriving Moslem-Christian town, with the pre-Vatican Council Romans completing their enormous, pretentious Church of the Annunciation alongside the narrow, smelly street where beggar boys still roam either inside or outside the arcades; with now a pretentious concrete Jewish quarter, to ensure that all Israel becomes Judaized. The holy places in Galilee have their moments—the churches of Tabor and Tabhga and the rest. And the Jewish guides contrive five loaves and two St. Peter fish, caught in Galilee, to follow Sunday morning communion by the sea.

It's clear enough. Jesus smelt this air and ran his fingers through this sand and fished in this lake and laughed with these boys and ate bread baked like this woman in Pequi'in bakes it now. Jesus went into the synagogue which is in ruins at Capernaum (or rather its predecessor), gave the Sermon on the Mount from this mount (or another, now over in Syria), and changed water into wine at Cana (this one or that). The pilgrim gets desperate at times. The "carpenter's shop," we demanded in Nazareth. Of course, of course, we will call on one on our way back. The owners do not quite see the joke as they stand up from their lathes and electric drills, busy producing modern doors for the rising modern flats, and gaze at our bewildered but almost anticipated disappointment.

So it was a mistake, after all, we surmise. We had come looking for places to be "close to him." We had come looking for an "experience." Sometimes, especially on the hillside or lakeside, or watching the peasants harvesting or the women bearing their burdens and the men on their donkeys (how long will they last in Israel?), there is an "experience." But the real conclusion is that Jesus was no "pale Galilean," no figure of sanctity, no man at the heights of experience. Humanly speaking—and how else can we speak?—Jesus was a working man who'd have given anything for an electric drill and a lathe, who sweated along these dusty roads and ignored the beggars as you have to now, who saw the cruelty of man to man and scarcely lifted a finger against it ("Render to Caesar" has been a cruel joke to some of his followers), who went out of his way to be problematic and even hostile to his family, his friends, his elders, his pastors, his rulers, and least acceptable of all, to his own mother and to the twelve men who, after all, had left everything and followed him. James Mitchell upset some Christians in 1966 when he described Jesus as "a defeated, muddled, superb and violent man, who some people thought was a little too fond of the bottle." [1] But it was an honest caricature.

It says nothing, either for faith or for devotion, to say that Jesus "lived as other men lived." That is not what we mean in talking of a "secular Christ." After all, I can drink the same tea, bathe in the same water supply, read the same books, use the same expletives as Mao Tse-Tung or the Queen of England. But that does not make me Mao Tse-Tung or the Queen, or make them any more like me.

It is rather what a man *does* in the situation of common humanity that distinguishes him. It is not the points at which

[1] *New Christian*, February, 1966.

Jesus was like us, but the points at which he was unlike us that are instructive. Not the points at which "miracle" intervenes, necessarily, but the points at which he or any man handles what we all do but handles it differently, handles it significantly, handles it in a sense *finally*—these are the points at which man betrays genius, lordship, or, one would guess, divinity.

The strangeness of Jesus is not his common humanity with us. His common humanity we have established for our century and take for granted—at least the people outside the churches do! The strangeness is something other.

The strangeness is in what he was that caused others to call him "Rabbi," "Master," "Lord," and even, afterwards, "God." The strangeness is in the arbitrariness, the oddness of this tiny incident in a backwater of the Roman Empire, which the historians hardly mention—that of becoming the faith and the life which overcame empires, which overcame religions, which overcame death. And it was not any *deus ex machina* that did it. It was *he!*

The theology of Christ is thus unashamedly *discriminatory*. By choosing to come as man, Jesus excluded womanhood (hence, of course, the divinization of Mary). By coming as a Galilean, Jesus excluded the Torah-obedient traditionalism of the rabbis. By belonging to the "pious poor" of the land, Jesus excluded the middle class and the beggars. By being a carpenter, Jesus excluded the rich and the wise. By preaching in Galilee, Jesus excluded the Judeans, let alone the Samaritans. By being a bachelor, Jesus excluded the insights of love and family. And so on.

These are what one might call the "accidentals," the things which do not explicitly form part of the gospel. They but emphasize the restriction, particularity, and selectiveness inherent in any human life. The church has not, in its best moments, read too much significance into these factors.

Yet they are absolutely unavoidably tied to the church's faith in "incarnation," or to any man's assessment of Jesus called the Christ.

The mission of Jesus is likewise discriminatory. By being baptized and preaching repentance, Jesus excluded the good who did not need repentance. By calling fishermen as disciples, Jesus excluded the student, the sage, or the rich. By healing the sick, Jesus excluded the young and the strong. By entertaining prostitutes and tax officials, Jesus excluded the decent middle classes. By disobeying the Law, Jesus excluded the Pharisees. By condemning the Temple, Jesus excluded the Sadducees and rulers. By excluding political allegiance, Jesus excluded Rome. By being crucified, Jesus excluded the hopes of Israel. There were odd exceptions to some of these. But in the main, it was true for Jesus as for us, that you can put your eggs into only one basket.

Now, what is all this about? Is it really that all those who did not get a look-in were rogues and rascals, or did not *need* the divine favor, or were too self-involved to see they needed it? Surely not!

But how do all the rest come in—particularly if they do not (as most of them do not) ever get to hear the gospel?

For all this is our subject—all this is the only material we have in trying to create a picture of Jesus or a theology of Jesus.

There is a strangeness in this story that can never fully be plumbed by theology or by life. There is a lasting fascination in this Jesus which will baffle man to the end of history. To write about Jesus is to write about this Jesus from the standpoint of one who does not believe it was all a sordid joke, who believes that ultimately "God is not mocked," and who is prepared with the earliest church to say that here, in this man, is more than meets the eye. But it will still remain a mystery. In fact, we would be happy if this book restores, for some people, the realm of mystery.

The Gospels know it. All that they say is that God was hidden in it and that God, in the end, "claimed" it for his own and told the unbelieving disciples that he had claimed it by the resurrection appearances; and by so doing, he let the whole extraordinary episode loose into the uttermost parts of creation, history, and human personality—the places which, in fact, had been the *loci* of Jesus, and the places to which he had pointed as being the places where the kingdom was hidden.

What it was—the whole thing about Jesus—we will now try to find out.

Chapter 6

MARK'S GOSPEL: A SECULAR JESUS

The stories of Jesus are almost exclusively contained in the four Gospels. They are a unique genre of literature. Their mutual relationship has been the source of prolonged discussion. We shall leave all this aside and seek, by a rapid survey of the earliest Gospel, Mark, to arrive at a general picture of the Gospel story, which will then be examined in more detail in the following chapters. We will confine ourselves in the present chapter to generally agreed on scholarly positions, although the shape and emphasis we see in the material will appear unavoidably even here.

Generally speaking, Mark's Gospel is held to be our earliest historical record for Jesus apart from references in Paul. The particular value of Mark within the early church traditions is that Mark's intention seems to be to show the historical ground, continuity, and meaning of the oral tradition which had existed from the days of Jesus himself.[1] When

---

[1] So esp. Julius Schniewind, *Das Markusevangelium* (Göttingen, 1953).

73

he takes over a story, or even groups of stories, from the tradition, he leaves it as it was, rarely adding comments, not even imposing a narrative form, and even allowing repetitions or doublets to remain.[2] Hence, he is a reliable witness to the earliest forms of the stories of Jesus, perhaps adding recollections of Peter. His Gospel abounds in lifelike and vivid touches, such as could have been derived from an eyewitness or eyewitnesses. According to Papias, as quoted in Eusebius (H.E. III. 39, 15), "Mark became the interpreter [translator?] of Peter, and wrote down accurately all he remembered of the words and deeds of the Lord, though not in order." Other references in early Christian literature link Mark with Peter, and provided we realize that this does not account for anything like the major part of this Gospel, we may accept the view that the author was Mark, the attendant of Peter, and that this Mark was also the John Mark of Acts. The Gospel is generally thought to have been written during A.D. 60-70, perhaps A.D. 65-66. Egypt, Antioch, and Rome are all suggested as places of origin. The latter seems the most likely.

Naturally, Mark reflects what interested him and his readers thirty years after Jesus' resurrection. But his apologetic concerns are confirmatory rather than corrective. He reflects, unpolemically, the liturgy (6:41, 8:6-7) and the topical and mnemonic methods of memorizing teaching in catechesis (4:21-5, 8:34–9:1, 9:37-50). However, he probably reflects later church dogmatic concern in his use of the title Son of God and in his elaboration of the miraculous and the apocalyptic elements.

[2] Vincent Taylor, ed., *The Gospel According to St. Mark* (New York: St. Martin's Press, 1952). For a more skeptical view, cf. D. E. Nineham, *The Gospel of St. Mark* (Baltimore: Pelican Books, 1964). C. E. B. Cranfield, ed., *The Gospel According to St. Mark* (Cambridge: Cambridge University Press, 1959), and the 16th ed. with the supplement of Ernst Lohmeyer, *Das Evangelium des Markus* (Berlin, 1963) are balanced and useful.

What, at any rate to me, is most striking about Mark is his obvious willingness to allow mysteries to remain mysteries and to pass on material which simply could not have been of use to the earliest churches, unless the thing they found most "useful" was to listen to the stories of Jesus, whether or not they could make anything of them.

As to its literary character, the Gospel has been analyzed in a variety of ways. It contains what have been described by the form critics as pronouncement stories (apothegms, paradigms), miracle stories, narratives about Jesus ("legends"), sayings and parables (especially in groups in chs. 4, 8, 11, and 13), and summary statements by the evangelist. Mark's arrangement of the material is mostly *topical*, in fairly brief sections. A good example of this is Mark 3:19-35, which brings together the story of Jesus "beside himself," the accusation of being possessed by Beelzebub, the sayings about the strong man bound, a saying about the Holy Spirit, and ends with a declaration of Jesus' true kindred, as against that referred to in vss. 19-21. This particular section may be historical as well as literary. Other typical "complexes" are 8:27-9:29, 10:1-31, and 11:27-12:44. Some seem to be based on existing tradition, some on personal testimony (Peter?), and some are merely literary complexes arranged topically.

This topical arrangement means that each incident is not necessarily in strict historical order, although the general order of events follows a logical and obviously historical sequence. The general plan of the Gospel is a simple enough one, suggesting eight divisions, which it may be useful to have in summary form.

(1) Introduction: The Gospel begins immediately with the baptism and temptation of Jesus (1:1-13). (2) Early Galilean ministry (1:14-3:6), including the call of the disciples, healing miracles, and first clashes over the Law. (3) Success in Galilee (3:7-6:13), leading to the appointment

of the twelve, charges against Jesus, Jesus' self-explanation by means of parables, and further miracles. (4) Beyond Galilee (6:14–8:26): Five thousand follow him and are fed, leading to the withdrawal to Tyre, the feeding of the four thousand, and the return to Bethsaida. (5) Toward Jerusalem (8:27–10:52): Jesus' disclosure of his impending destiny of suffering and its meaning with regard to discipleship, true greatness, riches, rewards, and personal life; and its status within God's history of salvation before (9:2-13), now (9:38-41), and after (10:28-31). (6) The Jerusalem ministry (11:1–13:37): Jesus enters Jerusalem; the barren fig tree and the Temple cleansing; teaching on true religion (ch. 12) and on the continuation of his sufferings in the church (ch. 13). (7) The passion (14:1–15:47): The plot, the Last Supper, the betrayal, trial, and mocking, the crucifixion and burial. (8) The resurrection (16:1-8): The empty tomb. The section 16:9-20, recording the appearances to Mary Magdalene, the two travelers, and to the eleven, and also recording the ascension, is not regarded as part of the original version of the Gospel.

However much this may look like a natural development in the actual story of Jesus, modern scholars are unanimous in believing that the Gospels are not "biographies" in the normal sense of the term. They were not written primarily to give a life story of Jesus but in order to demonstrate how and why the Christians believed that "all the secrets of life and death" had been opened up to man in Christ. Thus, Mark's work is a "theological" work, and it is not hard to see the picture of Jesus which he believed to be important and definitive. He sees the "good news" in what we may describe as three majestic contradictions: the humiliation of the Son of God, the battles of the love of God, and the presence of the *eschaton* of God.

(1) *The humiliation of the Son of God.* Mark's story is of a man who is not only a man, or man as no man was before (2:12). Jesus (81 times), the carpenter, the son of Mary (6:3), is yet called "rabbi," that is, "great one" (4 times), "teacher," "instructor" (12 times). The Son of God (5 times, but add 1:11, 9:7, 13:32) is yet hidden in the "son of man" (14 times). And as son of man he must suffer (9 of the "son of man" references are to the destiny of suffering) and yet will appear in glory (8:38, 13:26, 14:62). Jesus is proclaimed and anointed "Son of God" (1:11, and so forth), yet is moved by human sympathy (1:41), is angry (3:5), surprised (6:6), indignant (10:14), fearful (14:33). Jesus is the hidden God, the *deus mysterium.* He imposes secrecy (cf. Wrede!) because his "messiahship" (which Mark seeks to demonstrate) consists in the deeds and must be concluded and entered into when they have been acted and witnessed in their fullness.

(2) *The battles of the love of God.* The Father's love is basic to all that Jesus does. In Mark's atonement teaching (10:45, 14:24), there is no concept of appeasement, but rather of self-offering of God in man to God. The message of Mark is that God in the man Jesus battles with the forces of evil and overthrows them. Mark sees what Bultmann has called "the miraculous manifestation of divine healing cloaked in earthly occurrence." Once the *dynamis* of the Spirit takes possession of Jesus (1:12), he exorcises the devils (3:29), torments (5:7) and destroys them (1:26). The same pattern of this "exorcist" power overcoming evil is found in the nature miracles, debates with scribes and Pharisees (*Streitgespräche*), and in the discussions with the disciples.[3] God in

[3] So esp. J. M. Robinson, *The Problem of History in Mark* (Naperville, Ill.: Alec R. Allenson, 1957). Ernest Best, *The Temptation and the Passion* (Cambridge: Cambridge University Press, 1965), pp. 18-23, criticizes this, but one fears that this may be due to Best's own too systematic attempt to prove that Mark regarded Satan and the demons as overcome in the Temptation.

Jesus enters the human battles for existence and wholeness, and exerts his power to redeem men. This, as we shall see, means bringing out of every situation the essential question of life or death, communion or separation, meaning or futility, healing or possession. The disciple is called to enter into this decisive issue—not merely "decide" about it, but participate in it (3:15, 6:13, 9:18, 38 ff.; but also 8:32-33, 14:26-31).

(3) *The presence of the* eschaton *of God.* Mark understands the kingdom of God generally as future (14:25, 15:43), a state of God's rule to be brought in an apocalyptic manner (ch. 13). But it is also "at hand" (1:15) and present when the decisive character of Jesus' presence is realized (parables of ch. 4). It may be "received" now (10:15), though this is not as it is developed in Luke or Matthew. The kingdom impinges itself upon, casts its decisive shadow upon, the present every time the essential life-death issues are realized. The disciples' present self-discipline and stringency are their assurance of future possessions (10:29 ff.). Moreover, the community of the disciples already reflects some of the future blessings, as when their table fellowship looks back to the cross and forward to the parousia (14:22 ff.), and when the ordinary traditional life of Judaism is already set aside (2:23 ff., 3:1 ff.).[4]

What can be meant by calling this a "secular" Gospel? From our summary even so far, we see that Mark's purpose has been plainly to show that the life and ministry of Jesus on earth contained more than appeared on the surface—naturally, for Mark writes for those who, thirty years after, had never known Jesus "after the flesh"! Consequently, what we might call the nonsecular references are already beginning to be heightened. But his whole story is not about

[4] The presence of the kingdom, rather than of the Messiah, seems to me to be Mark's main burden. But cf. F. C. Grant, *The Earliest Gospel* (Nashville: Abingdon Press, 1953), pp. 148-74.

God, or heaven, or eternity, or ideas, or goodness, or providence, or anything else not available to ordinary man using his ordinary senses. His whole story is about Jesus, walking, talking, getting into boats, doing controversial things, healing, getting into arguments, evading opponents, securing friends, explaining himself, explaining his teaching. His whole story is about a *secular* event, an event within this world, which presupposes the limitations and opportunities of living in this world.

Thus secular as "that which pertains to this present, physical world" is a fair description. The whole story is "concerned with the affairs of this world, worldly, not sacred, . . . temporal, profane, lay" (Concise Oxford Dictionary).

But what about secular as "that which is separated from any metaphysical reference"? Is the whole story "sceptical of religious truth" (Concise Oxford Dictionary)? That will require a much more thorough examination of the way in which the secularity of Jesus contrives and indicates "something new" in the history of man and God.

Chapter 7

JESUS: A CHRISTOLOGY OF ACTION

In the last chapter we surveyed the Gospel of Mark and saw its essentially secular story. That same Gospel, however, was written by Christians for Christians. It reflects the faith of the earliest church. That church held certain beliefs about Jesus—it held him to be the Messiah, the Son of God, the Savior, the Lord. It had a very distinct Christology. Much of the work of Gospel scholarship is devoted to discovering how far these conceptions have influenced the way in which the Gospels now appear. We cannot go into details here. But we shall try to allow the evidence about Jesus to begin to question some of our presuppositions, so that what *it* has to tell us may appear, so that its own Christology may begin to emerge.

The question by which many people today would include or exclude themselves from the Christian faith is the simple one, "Is Jesus the Son of God?" Indeed, the World Council of Churches made its condition of membership to include "belief in Jesus Christ as God and Savior." Bultmann's voice seems to have been one of the few to question this statement.[1] In the main, the churches have presumably felt that this pocket Christology is a fair summary of Christian truth.

Yet, when one comes to inquire of the New Testament what exactly could be meant by this question, the evidence is rather different. Clearly, the Christian intention is to place Jesus in a "unique" relationship to God, a relationship not merely secured by Jesus from the human side, but also "given" to Jesus from the divine side. The earliest post-resurrection proclamation was that "God has made him both Lord (*Kurios*) and Christ (*Christos*; Hebrew *Messias*, Messiah), this Jesus whom you crucified" (Acts 2:36). The simpler form of this, "Jesus is Lord," or "Christ is Lord" (*Kurios Christos*), became the classic early Christian confession (cf. I Cor. 8:6, 12:3; Phil. 2:11; John 13:13).[2] The Gospel writers variously date the moment of Christ's acceptance by God, or God's claiming of Christ. Mark dates it to the baptism (Mark 1:11), Luke to the conception by the Holy Ghost (Luke 1:30-32), Matthew to the Davidic ancestry (Matt. 1:1-23), and John to the beginning of creation (John 1:1-12). Long ago, Pfleiderer argued a consistent New Testament Christology on the basis of these obvious facts,[3] and while I would not wish to follow all his arguments, it can nevertheless at least be claimed that this

[1] Rudolf Bultmann, *Essays Philosophical and Theological* (London: SCM Press, 1957), p. 273.

[2] Cf. Oscar Cullmann, *The Earliest Christian Confessions* (London: Lutterworth Press, 1949).

[3] Otto Pfleiderer, *The Early Christian Conception of Christ* (Williams & Norgate, 1905), pp. 16-20. The "Adoptionism" of Acts receives refreshing treatment recently in John Knox, *The Humanity and Divinity of Christ* (New York: Cambridge University Press, 1967); John Hick, "Christology at the Cross-Roads," in *Prospect for Theology: H. H. Farmer Festschrift* (Welwyn: James Nisbet, 1967), pp. 137-66; also to some extent, David E. Jenkins, *The Glory of Man* (New York: Charles Scribner's Sons, 1967). But I shall argue for a Christology latent in the Gospel actions, which in a sense require no "Adoption." But see also later, chapter 11 on the resurrection.

backdating corresponds to the sequence usually given to the chronology of the Gospel writings and contains within it a certain natural, psychological argument.

More recently, Christology has been written in terms of the titles applied to Jesus, as if certain titles could be regarded as being used roughly with the same intention, whoever the author or whatever the time or circumstance of writing. The most outstanding recent work along this line is that of Oscar Cullmann[4] and Vincent Taylor.[5] The other way to approach the christological material, pioneered by Bultmann, has been lately followed by R. H. Fuller,[6] who attempts to show how the christological titles used for Jesus in the New Testament derive from various situations—those of early Jewish Christianity, the Hellenistic church, or the developed church. Unfortunately, the existence of these varieties of influence has never been demonstrated, so that any historical development worked out using them as basic ingredients is fraught with difficulties, of which Fuller is certainly aware.

Again, there is a tendency for much Gospel scholarship to assume that Jesus had a set of titles before him and was choosing which of them he would be known by. Books are still being written about whether Jesus thought of himself as the son of man, or the Suffering Servant of Isaiah 53, or the Son of God, or the Christ, as if these were settled notions in men's minds and all that Jesus had to say was, "Yes, I am that," or "No, I am not that," or "I will do this to show what I am." Doubtless, the liberal search for the "self-consciousness" of Jesus cannot be revived in its old form. Nevertheless, the rigid adherence to any one title, or any

[4] *The Christology of the New Testament* (Philadelphia: The Westminster Press, 1964).

[5] *The Names of Jesus* (New York: St. Martins Press, 1953) and *The Person of Christ* (St. Martins Press, 1958).

[6] *The Foundations of New Testament Christology* (New York: Charles Scribner's Sons, 1965).

combination of them, makes nonsense of the Gospel accounts which mainly record healings, teachings, miracles, debates, training of disciples, and so forth—none of which belonged essentially to any of the figures mentioned. A rigid adherence to any one or more titles also gravely oversimplifies Jesus' own conception of his work, and the simplification shows him to have believed himself to be one thing, but to have spent most of his time doing others.

In fact, the christological search as a · debate concerning titles has effectively prevented scholars of our age from discerning certain "lines" which are authentic to Judaism and which can, in fact, be exhibited in Jesus. Some of them are present in the frequently neglected intertestamental literature, the Wisdom writings. Some of them are utilized in the Qumran documents to describe the "teacher of righteousness," or more correctly, the "right teacher."

One "line" is that of the Old Testament picture of the truly righteous man, the pious good man of the Psalms, who becomes in Isaiah the man whose goodness survives suffering, and in Maccabees, the man whose good death has vicarious value for others. When Jesus calls his disciples to the way of the beatitudes (Matt. 5:1-16), which implies suffering, he calls them to follow this way which he himself treads. Another "line" not dissimilar is that of the figure seen variously as the Torah-obedient man, the wise man, the embodiment of wisdom, a figure akin to the Greek philosopher-preacher. When Jesus calls disciples to him and shows them the "secrets of the kingdom" and teaches them to learn them,[7] he calls them not to be the disciples of the Messiah, but to be the disciples of a Rabbi, a Teacher, who as such becomes known as "Master." (The Greek *Kurios* is a natural development, if not translation, of the Aramaic *Rab*, teacher, and *Mar*,

[7] Cf. my paper, "Did Jesus Teach His Disciples to Learn by Heart?" in *Studia Evangelica*, III (Berlin, 1964), 105-18.

master.). Another "line" is that of the possibility of a new Torah, heralding or preparing for the messianic time. Jesus, by setting aside the old Law and replacing it with obedience to himself, inevitably raises the question: What is this—a new Law? (*Kaine didache,* Mark 1:27).

Three comments must be made, however. First, each of these lines is not a question of titles but of *actions* of Jesus, which he then justifies and explains by words. Second, each of these lines is not an *isolated* matter relating to the uniqueness of Jesus, but rather is something larger, to which he himself is related or "discipled," and to which his followers also become discipled through following him. Third, Jesus is not "determined" in his actions by any of these lines, any more than he is by titles with which New Testament scholarship juggles. Jesus does what he does, and man must make the best of it. But these "lines" do illuminate his words and deeds more clearly than the old method of titles.[8]

The Gospels themselves, indeed, frequently display a rather alarming lack of concern about the titles being used. Moreover, we find an insistence on the part of Jesus, particularly in the early part of Mark, that no title can be used of him. The *basic* answer of the New Testament is in Johannine language: See Jesus and you have seen it all—Father, heaven, way, truth, and life. Look at Jesus, for he is the one who uniquely, representatively, finds favor and acceptance with God. But this answer is given by the New Testament in such varied and diverse forms that it cannot be simply reduced to a "yes" or "no" to the question: Was Jesus divine?

The Gospels, as we have seen, are not primarily answers to questions but are attempts to find man's feet in the light of Jesus. You cannot ask: Is Jesus the Son of God? You can

---

[8] This I hope to show in *Disciple and Lord.* My Basel doctoral dissertation (1960) on "Discipleship in the Synoptic Gospels as a Historical and Theological Problem" formed the basis for this study.

ask: What does a man, filled with the spirit of God, do? And then, you must allow the New Testament to tell its own story and not be influenced, or at least determined, by the questions being raised about Jesus, either by his own contemporaries or by men today. Jesus was an enigma to his own family. He was rejected by those who knew or thought they knew (and indeed all the evidence goes to show that the scribes, Pharisees, and the rest did know) what was *supposed* to be God's manifestation on earth in the person of his anointed one. He was misunderstood, doubted, and rejected by his own disciples. There is a great temptation for Christians to want to be wiser than all of them. The writers of the Gospels, however, do not claim to be wiser than all of them. And there is, indeed, no way in which we can come to Christ from the outside and make anything of the story at all, in terms of "titles," and "conclusions." There is no reason why modern contemporary man should think that because he comes with questions that are important to him, he will necessarily be any more successful in recognizing Jesus as the Messiah than the scribes and Pharisees—with their preconceived ideas of what they were looking for—or his own disciples, or his own family.

The typical answer of the Gospels to the questions: What is Jesus? and Who is Jesus? and What is supposed to be going on? is evoked by the question of John the Baptist. John had hailed Jesus at the baptism and heard the voice from heaven, "This is my beloved Son. Listen to him." Then John was put in jail and sent two of his disciples to Jesus to ask, "Are you the one who is to come, or are we to expect some other?" (Luke 7:19 NEB). This is a somewhat amazing question, amazing in that the Gospel writers should include it in this way. John, after all, was in prison and in danger of his life, and the whole of his ministry he had allowed to be understood as merely preparation for the coming one. And now he was beginning to have doubts: Is Jesus the one who was to come, or are we to go on expecting someone else? The questioners come and ask their question to Jesus Christ. And there and then Jesus "cured many sufferers from diseases, plagues, and evil spirits; and on many blind people he bestowed sight" (vs. 21). At last, he gave them his answer:

Go and tell John what you have seen and heard: how the blind recover their sight, the lame walk, the lepers are clean, the deaf hear, the dead are raised to life, the poor are hearing the good news —and happy is the man who does not find me a stumbling-block. (Luke 7:22-23 NEB.)

Basically, this is the only answer of Jesus Christ to the question of who he is, or to the question about what he is doing. He is what he is, and he does what he does. He is what he is because he is God's anointed. He does what he does because they are the deeds he has to do as God's anointed. If we try to pry further, there is no answer, but simply, "Happy is the man who does not find me a stumbling-block." There is every reason and excuse for the man who stumbles. There is "no beauty that we should desire him," as Isaiah 53:2 has it. No man with any kind of preconception about what he will find in Christ in fact finds the Christ in Jesus. Jesus quite deliberately avoids any kind of conclusion to his work, which could be summed up in such a phrase as "You are the Son of God," or "You are the Messiah." It may be thought that the confession of Peter at Caesarea Philippi goes against this (Mark 8:29). But Jesus follows this curious exchange by telling Peter that he represents Satan and by commanding absolute silence. In other words, the story of Peter's confession has to be seen in the light of the whole evidence of the Gospels, and not the whole evidence of the Gospels seen in the light of that one incident, as has been the case with much

British scholarship, from T. W. Manson onward.[9] Moreover, in any case, if one puts one's emphasis there, one must immediately go on to show how Jesus described his destiny in terms of suffering and death, which is quite irreconcilable with the usual idea of the "anointed one."

Jesus is saying that no one who brings any kind of preconceptions with him can discover who he, Jesus, is. But there is much more. Jesus is also saying that it is not man's questions to him that are important. Rather, man must open himself to the new set of questions about man's existence being posed by Jesus' presence over against him. Man's own questions to Jesus are so often avoided, or answered in different terms, simply because man's own questions allow him to hide from the fact that Jesus' own existence before him puts the man himself in question. Jesus is the questioner, and only when man has stumbled at, or loved, the peculiarity of Jesus, is there any place for his questions. This is constantly evident in the parables and in Jesus' dealings with people who come objecting to this, that, or the other in the scandalously extreme and extraordinary which man finds in the words and deeds of Jesus. "Happy is the man who does not find me a stumbling-block."

What is the purpose of the Gospels allowing Jesus to be so "unhelpful"? Surely it is because Christology hangs upon the action of Jesus and the action of the questioner. The ultimate answer of Jesus to questions about himself is always another question: Are you the kind of person who can see—in blind people seeing, lame people walking, deaf people hearing, dead people living, poor people listening to the good news —the actual living presence of that which is messianic, that which is sealed and anointed by God?

And that is still, we may add immediately, basically the

[9] *The Teaching of Jesus* (Cambridge: Cambridge University Press, 1931), pp. 201-11.

question of the synoptic Jesus in reply to modern man's question: What is Christ for man today? Perhaps, in any case, the question could easily be merely inquisitorial; it is not basically "Christ" whom we look for, any of us, if we are honest. But whether this is so or not, we must understand that our existence has been called into question by Christ, and we can only see God's anointing resting on Jesus if we are prepared to be scandalized, shocked, "caught out" by it. *We*, not Christ, are being judged. We are being judged by our ability to see in the deeds of Jesus that which could possibly be God resting his blessing upon human existence. The deeds of Jesus are really not what we came looking for, either as an assessment of human existence at its best or as a manifestation of a powerful God. But that is all there is for us to find.

There is indeed a Christology in the Gospels, a very high Christology. But it is a Christology quite different from the one we formulate if we begin with titles. The interminable discussion about titles perhaps suggests that there is no final answer to such questions. What the Gospels claim, as we shall see in the next chapter, is that Jesus is Lord or Master, and that he goes about his business, right from the beginning, as if he were God Almighty. This is the difficulty that the scribes and Pharisees find in him when they observe him healing and, by the same token, forgiving sins: "Who can forgive sins on earth, save God alone?" And Jesus remains silent because the scribes and Pharisees have observed precisely the thing which is the whole object of the operation, notably that God is now no longer performing his actions in heaven because Jesus is doing them on earth.

Now, there cannot be a higher Christology than this, but it is not a Christology of titles. It is a Christology which makes us conclude: Jesus is the Son of God or Jesus is the son of man or Jesus is the Christ. If we wanted to find terms for it, we would have to say, as we shall suggest, that Jesus is the secular activity of the hidden God. And it is precisely this *action* of Jesus, not any "claim" of Jesus, which causes the scribes and Pharisees to conclude that he is making himself out to be God. This is exactly what the Gospel writers are saying—that Jesus is God Incarnate, that Jesus is acting on earth as if he were God.

Is there any proof of this "acting as if he were God" apart from the deeds? Ethelbert Stauffer has suggested that when Jesus told his frightened disciples, "I am he"—"It is I," on the lake of Galilee (Mark 6:45-52), he was using the mysterious name of God himself—ANI HU, "I am he." Stauffer refers to Mark 13:6: "Many will come . . . saying, 'ANI HU,'" and to Mark 14:62, where Caiaphas nails it down as blasphemy. The theory is unlikely to be correct, even though we may admit that John might have had such a scheme (John 4:26, 6:16 ff., 8:24 ff., 13:19) and even though the Jewish sources which Stauffer quotes are fascinating. But what Stauffer *means* by "I am he" has been said adequately in Mark, without recourse to this divine revelatory formula, and Stauffer is right in putting into the mouth of Jesus the assertions: "Where I am, there is God, there God lives, speaks, calls, asks, acts, decides, loves, chooses, forgives, rejects, hardens, suffers, dies. Nothing bolder can be said, or imagined." [10] This is not a "claim" of Jesus; it is just that he acts as if it were true and compels man to draw new conclusions in the light of the evidence. Jesus does not "claim" to be anything; he just acts in a way in which no man has ever acted before. His actions *constitute* his status before man and therefore compel man into decision. His actions *constitute* his status before God and ultimately are shown to be the accepted deeds of God. His actions are the actions of a human being, a man in a human situation. Jesus does not cease to be man when his

[10] *Jesus and His Story* (New York: Alfred A. Knopf, 1960), p. 159.

actions are seen to be the actions also of God. As Bonhoeffer puts it:

The statement "This man is God" touches on Jesus vertically from above. It takes nothing from him and adds nothing to him. It simply qualifies the whole man Jesus as God. It is God's judgment and Word on this man.[11]

And even this "Word of God coming from above," Bonhoeffer goes on, is not "something which is added," but rather "is in fact the man Jesus Christ himself," who "*is* also God's judgment on himself."

At the end of the last chapter we observed two meanings of the overworked word "secular." In the first place, it could indicate Jesus as an ordinary human being, in the midst of the situation of the world. But it could also mean "separated from any metaphysical reference." So far, our answer in this sense must be equivocal. A metaphysical framework is not needed in coming to the evidence about Jesus. Indeed, any kind of framework will probably be an embarrassment—either that, or Jesus will be the embarrassment! But does Jesus have a "metaphysical reference"? Rarely are we given any hint of this.

What are we to say about Jesus, then?

For the moment we must caution ourselves against wanting to put Jesus too quickly within a framework which *we* think will give him significance (or "divinity"), but which will prevent the impact of what he really was and did from coming upon us. Erik Routley has entered a vigorous protest against what he calls the "uncontexted Christ." Routley says, "We simply must not extract Him from his context—from

[11] Dietrich Bonhoeffer, *Christ the Center* (New York: Harper & Row, 1966), p. 107. Published in England as *Christology* (London: William Collins Sons, 1966).

the Messianic function of reconciliation." [12] Yet, we cannot help asking whether Routley's "context" is the right one, the only one, or the one which would most naturally suggest itself to a reader of the Gospels.

We shall conclude this chapter by mentioning, by way of caution, three typical ways of thinking of Jesus, which have arisen out of Christian devotion, both in New Testament days and in modern days, but which we must beware of if we are to let the "strangeness of Jesus" compel us to decisions of a new kind.

(1) *Preconceptions about sin and sinlessness.* Much Christian thinking begins with the cross of Christ, and this emphasis upon the passion almost always means that one "reads back" a picture of the human Jesus in order to fit it. Thus, Paul in Romans speaks of the cross as a "right-making" action (Rom. 5:1-21), which demands that the Gospels shall describe a man who is always "right." In fact, they do no such thing, and Jesus refuses even to call himself good. The New Testament theology of the cross speaks of a perfect sin offering, a "lamb without blemish," which demands that the Gospels shall describe one who is sinless, without blemish. Again, they do no such thing, as is shown in Jesus' anger at the money changers, his harshness to his mother, his evasions of his enemies, his breaking the Law of his people, his stirring up revolt against the rulers and religious men of his country.

Why all this? Not, I venture to think—as Bonhoeffer, who gives the list, claims—because Jesus "entered man's sinful existence *past recognition.*" There is, in fact, no picture of "man's sinful existence" in the Gospels; that is to bring a theology of the cross into the picture which demands a sinner/sinless dichotomy—a sinless dying for the sinful. Indeed, Bonhoeffer later says as much:

[12] *The Man for Others* (Gloucester, Mass.: Peter Smith, 1964), p. 79.

The assertion of the sinlessness of Jesus fails if it has in mind observable acts of Jesus. His deeds are done in the likeness of flesh. They are not sinless, but ambiguous. One can and should see good and bad in them.[13]

No, the sinless man, the pious man, the righteous man, does *not* act as Jesus acts.

There is, again, no reason—except a similar back-reading of Pauline theology—for saying that Jesus remained "sinless" but yet took "sinful flesh." [14] Apart from the difficulty that this makes sinful flesh into some kind of abstraction, "whereas sin is rather a possibility in which a concrete existent stands," [15] it also introduces categories quite foreign to those either in the Gospels, or suggested naturally by the Gospels. "Incarnation," as we shall see, becomes a rather confusing category when divorced from the actual Gospel story, quite apart from its "metaphysical" presuppositions.

(2) *Preconceptions of Jesus as the devotional model.* There is little evidence in Mark for the much-quoted notion of Jesus' constant personal communion in prayer with his Father. Jesus is simply proclaimed in baptism to be "God's beloved," and proceeds to act on earth as God does in heaven. Luke systematizes the times of withdrawal for prayer into a scheme whereby Jesus withdraws for prayer usually just prior to some great turning point or decision. But, in fact, this only serves to illustrate the Gospel's secular slant. Prayer in the Gospels is always for something particular, and not simply communion with God. Luke 11:1-12 makes this plain, for Luke follows the Lord's Prayer with the parable of the man waking up his friend at midnight and making a din until he

[13] Bonhoeffer, *Christ the Center*, pp. 112-13.

[14] John Knox, *The Church and the Reality of Christ* (New York: Harper & Row, 1962), p. 135.

[15] John Macquarrie, *Studies in Christian Existentialism* (Philadelphia: The Westminster Press, 1966), p. 241.

gets what he wants. "Keep on asking for what you want until you get it" is the message. Prayer in the Gospels is mundane, entirely related to securing "secular" ends, and not communion with God.[16]

There is, of course, a simple presupposition that God exists, like any other person. But man's dealings with him are always of this mundane, realistic nature. Jesus' reference to God as Father, *Abba*, was a realistic relationship to one whom he believed to be "with him" and was based on what he was doing; it was not a cry into the heavens or a "personal friendship" with a "spiritual" God. The later Gospels, and especially the apocryphal ones, heighten all references to Jesus as a "spiritual" man, but this is because of the Gnostic and Encratite influences that emerged in the second half of the first century, which sought to eliminate the worldly and material side of Jesus' character.

(3) *Preconceptions of Jesus as "Messiah."* What of the claim that Jesus is the "Messiah," the "Christ" of Jewish expectation? Certainly, Mark's Gospel is written by one who sought to show that Jesus was God's anointed one. But, to say that Jesus was Messiah—or was not—is to bring into the discussion a static notion of an "expected one," which is simply not to be found in first-century Judaism.

To begin with, it has long been debated whether the idea of a Messiah was or was not current in Israel in the time of Christ. Recently, several factors have suggested that it probably was not. First, the notion of anointed one, often related to prophet, priest, or king, is certainly not usually identified with the deliverer of whom we hear in the apocalyptic writings.[17] Second, we do not know the relationship of the

---

[16] Cf. also Günther Bornkamm, *Jesus of Nazareth* (New York: Harper & Row, 1960), p. 134. In general, cf. Eduard Schweizer, *Lordship and Discipleship* (Naperville, Ill.: Alec R. Allenson, 1960).

[17] M. de Jonge ("The Use of the Word 'Anointed' in the Time of Jesus," *Novum Testamentum*, VIII [1966], 132-48) argues that "anointed one" was

notion of an anointed one to the later codified expectations either of a "messianic age" or of the "age to come" (the two were differentiated).

The Dead Sea Scrolls have further illustrated the confusion. The Manual of Discipline, chapter 9, expects three messianic figures: the Prophet, the Messiah of Aaron, and the Messiah of Israel. In other parts of the Scrolls and in the Damascus Document, things become even more complicated.[18] In these communities we have a very special kind of expectation, and while it is still fashionable to call the monks of Qumran "sectarians" and even "heretics," we simply do not know what constituted "orthodoxy" in the first part of the first century. We know what *became* orthodoxy after the fall of Jerusalem in A.D. 70, when the rabbis gathered together at the Council of Jamnia (A.D. 84) to codify what they could of the traditions of Judaism. That codification of Judaism, in fact, is remarkably unmessianic in places, and we have no grounds for saying that this was necessarily out of reaction against Christianity. Insofar as there are codified lists of messianic characteristics, the Jew of any age has little difficulty in showing that Jesus does not "fit the bill." The Jewish scholar Isaak Troki (1533-94) lists twenty-six curious characteristics of the OT messianic hope which Jesus did not fulfill.

Neither can it be demonstrated that the Gospel evidence concerning Jesus as Messiah is plain or unequivocal. In some respects, what happens in the Gospel story is much more like the "age to come" than it is like the Messiah's time, for the Messiah only heralded the Day of the Lord, whereas Jesus

---

not an essential part of Jewish eschatological thinking, that it was not a designation essential to a future redeemer, and that "not the person as such, but his calling and his function are of importance. Nothing is said about the duration of the period of his activity as an instrument of God."

[18] Cf. Géza Vermès, *The Dead Sea Scrolls in English* (Baltimore: Penguin Books, 1962), pp. 47-51; A. R. C. Leaney, *The Rule of Qumran and Its Meaning* (Philadelphia: The Westminster Press, 1966), pp. 215 ff.

actually brought it. C. F. D. Moule has suggested that in Mark 12:36 Jesus used psalm 110 to indicate that what was true of the Christ would be even more true of a more-than-Christ—the Lord.

Thus, it is arguable that Jesus conceived of John as Elijah (which places John on the level of the Messiah as ordinarily conceived), but saw his own function as equivalent not to the Messiah as ordinarily conceived but to more than the Messiah—indeed to that which Elijah (or the Messiah) heralds. Elijah heralds the Day of the Lord. If Jesus' herald, John the Baptist, is Elijah, then the coming of Jesus himself is tantamount to the coming of the Day of the Lord.[19]

All we can say is that if there is a claim that Jesus is God's anointed, Messiah, it can only be that *this one* in the Gospel story who "is what he is" and "does what he does" is in fact the one of whom God shows his approval. But we can never prove that Jesus was the Messiah. God just believed in him.[20]

What, then, is the *distinctive* thing about the Jesus-story?

The ancient world abounds in stories of gods appearing in human guise, of miracle workers, of philosopher-teachers, of leaders of communistic movements into the desert, of champions of popular piety against organized religion, of radical prophets against the establishment, of "messiahs" claimed or self-styled. There are points of contact between Jesus and all of these, and many of them are extremely illuminating. Indeed, the apologists of the second century and since have succeeded in arguing that Jesus is the fulfillment of them all, each age emphasizing that element which seemed most relevant at the time.

Yet is any of them the *distinctive* thing about the Jesus-story?

[19] *The Phenomenon of the New Testament,* pp. 71-72.
[20] Cf. Geoffrey Ainger, *Jesus Our Contemporary* (New York: The Seabury Press, 1967), pp. 66-67.

Chapter 8

MINISTRY: THE HEALING OF THE KINGDOM

If we refuse to give a simple answer to the questions: Who is Christ? and What is Christ? and insist on the tautological, "he is what he is," this drives us to the Gospels to discover "all that Jesus began to do and teach" (Acts 1:1) as the one and only clue or authentication of "theology."

Obviously, we cannot consider all the evidence, even in Mark's Gospel, in detail. Nor yet do we need to do so. For the main theological and christological interests of the Gospel can be derived even from a study of a small part of it. We propose, therefore, to take our question: What is Jesus doing? to the first two chapters of Mark, in particular chapter 2. We shall not delay to deal with critical points but will concern ourselves with Mark's theological purpose. There is, in fact, no good reason to question the basic historicity of these particular passages.[1]

According to Mark, it was on the secular level that expecta-

[1] Cf. in general, L. E. Keck, "The Introduction to Mark's Gospel," *New Testament Studies*, XII (1965-1966), 352-70.

tion of a deliverer ran high when Jesus arrived on the scene. "Are you the one who is to redeem Israel?" they had asked of the Maccabees, the zealot leaders, of Judas the Galilean. They asked it of Jesus. They meant by it someone who would deliver them from the Romans and reestablish the ancient laws and customs of Israel (Luke 24:21).

At the beginning, it seemed that there could be hope that Jesus was the one. He is baptized in Jordan, and Mark understands this not as a separation from mankind for a special function, but as a baptism into mankind of one who now stands within humanity as "My Son, my beloved." This anointing of Jesus by baptism and by the Spirit imparts a divine commission to Jesus which he now sets about carrying out.

Thus, Jesus emerges from his baptism as the anointed (*Messias*) to do God's work. He gives himself unhesitatingly to a vocation determined by the nearness of a "kingdom." And that kingdom is here on this earth, a secular kingdom. "Repent, it's here," he cries, and immediately sets about gathering his followers around him. "Follow me and I will make you become fishers of men," he says (Mark 1:17). Whatever that curious phrase may mean—and there are at least four possibilities—one cannot help observing that fish which have been caught are lifted out of the water and do not live any longer. Whatever the figure means, it implies a pretty drastic change in any man's existence! The secular world now has the kingdom of God in the midst of it, because of Jesus and proclaimed by Jesus.

The whole of the earthly part of Jesus' ministry, in a sense, is conducted in a thoroughly "secular" way. That is to say, Jesus is the one on whom God's favor rests, and he is able to command the evil spirits and they obey him. There is no question of any constant reference to the supernatural or to God (John's Gospel alters this, of course). Jesus has the power (*exousia*) necessary and gets on with the job. He does it because of what God has made him—his anointed one. Inasmuch as Jesus stands in relation to this anointing, there is a metaphysical reference. But it is a reference that is essentially hidden from all human analysis. It is quite sufficient for men to see the deeds and by faith to become involved in them either as recipients (in the case of healing) or as participants (in the case of discipleship).

How does it happen? Three important discussions in the second chapter of Mark fill out the picture.

(1) *The discussion on forgiveness and healing.*

Which is easier, to say to the paralytic, "Your sins are forgiven," or to say, "Rise, take up your pallet and walk"? But that you may know that the Son of man has authority on earth to forgive sins— he said to the paralytic—I say to you, rise, take your pallet and go home." (Mark 2:9-11.)

On the surface, it is easier to forgive sins. That is to say, no external and irrefutable proof is required that forgiveness has been effected. But with healing there is an external and irrefutable proof. Jesus is prepared to submit to the factual test, the test whether the man will get up. This is the proof that forgiveness has taken place. The healing is a sign that the man's sins were forgiven. Forgiveness without healing would have been irrelevant; healing without forgiveness would have been impossible. The only thing with which the lawyers were concerned was the forgiving, which was regarded as the sole prerogative of God. Healing could have been performed by many people. It is interesting how the modern reader boggles at the healing and accepts the forgiving without question—the exact opposite of the attitude of Jesus' contemporaries.

Mark wishes to tell us three things about what Jesus does

here. First, Jesus arrogates to himself the prerogative of God. Jesus simply sees the faith of the men who lower the paralytic and says to him, "My son, your sins are forgiven." That is to say, Jesus acts on earth in an earthly situation as if he were God in heaven. He says that the thing that God in heaven does is now being done by him on earth. This is why the lawyers accuse him of blasphemy—and not without reason. This is the whole point of the story. God's actions are no longer being done in heaven. They are being done on earth by this man Jesus. The source called Q reads, "If I by the finger of God cast out devils, then the kingdom of God has come near to you" (cf. Luke 11:20; Matt. 12:28).

Second, Jesus identifies "Rise, take up your bed and walk" with "Your sins are forgiven." This can be the only possible meaning behind the discussion of which is easier. It is indeed *easier* to say, simply, "Son, your sins are forgiven," than to say, "Take up your bed and walk." But it is essentially the same thing. To forgive is to heal, and to heal is to forgive. That is to say, the healing is the present and efficacious action whereby the divine prerogative of forgiveness is appropriated by Jesus and whereby the paralytic is restored. The earthly, mundane act of healing the body is the act whereby the divine forgiveness now available in Jesus is communicated. The healing of Jesus is not simply something which could be done by others. It is a *sign* of what now can be done by him "in place of God"—notably, the forgiving of sins.

Third, there is the claim that "the son of man has the power on earth (as distinct from heaven, which remains God's province?) to forgive sins" (vs. 10). We shall return to the meaning of "son of man" in a moment.

(2) *The meals with publicans and sinners.*

Immediately following this healing miracle, Mark records that Jesus called Levi at his seat in the custom house, and went home with him to a meal, at which other tax gatherers and evil doers sat with Jesus and his disciples (Mark 2:14 ff.). When the scribes of the Pharisees complain, Jesus replies: "Those who are well have no need of a physician, but those who are sick; I came not to call the righteous, but sinners" (vs. 17). The publicans were traitors to their country, *collaborateurs*, extortioners, unjust, whose contact with the gentile Romans rendered them outside the pale of the Law. The "sinners" could be anyone who did not belong to the strict parties which adhered to the Law, either because they lived immoral lives or because they had degrading occupations. They were simply the *'am ha-arez*, the people of the land, the multitude "who do not know the law," who are "accursed" (John 7:49).

What could have been meant by Jesus seeking out this embarrassing and unsavory company? It seems to have been a settled policy, as shown by his selection of Zacchaeus (Luke 19:1-10) and the frequent criticisms of his bad company. It clearly did not confine itself to men. It extended to women. It extended to practicing prostitutes. Matt. 21:28-31 even says that practicing tax gatherers and prostitutes go into heaven before the (self-styled?) righteous! [2]

What does Mark mean to tell us by all this?

It is not an accidental story. It is part of what Jesus is doing concerning the kingdom. Jesus has *opened* the kingdom of heaven, and the symbol of the kingdom is a banquet, as in the "great banquet" (Luke 14:16 ff.) or the marriage feast of the king's son (Matt. 22:2 ff.) or the feast in the ten virgins parable (Matt. 25:1-13) or the feast for the returning prodigal (Luke 15:23-32). A meal is the figure of the kingdom of God (*basileia tou theou*) (Luke 14:15; Matt. 8:11-13). In all these illustrations, it becomes clear that the king-

[2] Norman Perrin, *Rediscovering the Teaching of Jesus* (New York: Harper & Row 1967), pp. 102-108, sees the table fellowship as the "central feature of the ministry of Jesus."

dom meal does not simply remain a "picture" of a future celebration. The celebration is now possible, and Jesus acts this out by his own actions. By eating with publicans and sinners, by feeding the five thousand, by acting as host in the Pharisee's house, by being head of the table to his disciples, Jesus symbolically represents the king at the banquet, God in his kingdom. Such a celebration belongs to this time, when God's deeds are being done on earth! And, at the end, Jesus tells his disciples that he will not do it again until he does it "in the kingdom"! (Mark 14:25; Luke 22:16, 18; Matt. 26:29.)

The kingdom thus becomes dynamically present, even if only momentarily, in the deeds of Jesus. The Hebrew word for kingdom, *malkuth*, can be used either of a kingdom meaning an area of rule, or it can be used to mean the act of ruling, the place where rule appears. In the Gospels, in the sense that the kingdom has come (Mark 1:15), it is obviously used in the latter sense. Insofar as there are places through the work of Jesus where the "dynamite" which is God's rule becomes active, the kingdom *has* come, as lightning suddenly descends. This is not the only form in which the kingdom is to appear, but it is the form dynamically represented in the healing and exorcism ministries of Jesus.[3]

But, by saying that Jesus has opened the kingdom of God, Mark can only mean that God has allowed his kingdom to be opened, God has allowed his lightning to descend, his hidden rule to appear through the deeds of Jesus. It means that Jesus is acting as if he had a warrant from the King to act in his place in his kingdom!

We may go further.

The whole tradition of Jesus seeking and saving the lost (Luke 19:10) implies that Jesus acts as if he is God. If he

[3] Cf. George E. Ladd, *Jesus and the Kingdom* (New York: Harper & Row, 1964), pp. 145-60; q.v. for other literature.

were a good man, he would know what kind of people these prostitutes and sinners are (Luke 7:39, 19:7) and would have nothing to do with them. Jesus is content, however, that this shall be thought of him because, as he says, he is not a "good" man (Mark 10:18). The Gospel writers do not seem to know anything of any divine self-consciousness of Jesus. They know of the deeds, though, and by the deeds, Jesus imitates the deeds of God. He bypasses human notions of goodness. He presumes to act as God. One of the deeds of God is forgiveness. Another is merciful loving-kindness. These things, ideally, are enshrined in the Law of the Old Testament, the Torah. There the Jew learned that he was expected to imitate the deeds of God. But now, in Jesus, the mercy and loving-kindness of God, his *chesed*, overflow and become impossible and irresponsible. Through the person of Jesus, God loses himself and his "attributes"!

(3) *The disciples, the old Law and the new Law.*

The rest of Mark 2 is concerned with the old Law and the inevitability of its irrelevance for life in the present situation. The disciples are criticized for not fasting, and Jesus replies that you can hardly expect the bridegroom's mates to fast when the wedding party is on (Mark 2:18-20). There is new wine around and you will only ruin both the new wine and the old skins if you try to put one in the other (vss. 21-22). The disciples are as much entitled to eat corn on the sabbath as David and his men were to eat the consecrated loaves (vss. 23-26). Moreover, since the sabbath was made for man and not man for the sabbath, the "son of man" is Lord over the sabbath (vss. 27-28).

Four comments are relevant to our purpose. First, Mark, as he does so often, sets a discussion on the permissibles in the new human situation in the face of Jesus Christ, within the context of eating and drinking. There's a party on. Don't expect the guests to fast. Don't expect to use old wineskins.

And it doesn't matter if bread is eaten on the sabbath—or even (presumably), "consecrated loaves" (NEB: *tous artous tes protheseos*). If a man is hungry, then he must eat—particularly now that men have the kingdom butting in upon them.

Second, let us examine the term "son of man." We have so far written this term as "son of man" because to use capital letters for it implies that a definite personage (usually regarded as semidivine) with a title is intended.[4] We will now say a little about it. In reading Mark 2:27-28, it is evident that the "son of man" is obviously either any man whatsoever or else a generic term covering the disciples in this instance. T. W. Manson thought this a good text to justify his "corporate" interpretation of the son of man sayings.[5] However, there are few scholars who follow him in this. The two most recent studies of the son of man—by H. E. Tödt and A. J. B. Higgins[6]—have both argued that only the futuristic sayings concerning the son of man are genuine and that the sayings referring to the present work of Jesus and those referring to his impending passion are secondary. With the second of these judgments there has been some agreement for some time, though every text must be taken on its own merits.

Regarding the son of man sayings which refer to the present work of Jesus, it seems to me that many more problems are created by removing them all than by asking some

---

[4] Géza Vermès, in a paper at the Oxford New Testament Congress of 1965, has questioned whether *bar nashar* was ever used in a titular sense in Jewish-Aramaic, although the word itself does occur in a nontitular sense in early Galilean Aramaic. See Appendix to Matthew Black, *Aramaic Approach to the Gospels and Acts* (3rd. ed.; Oxford: Oxford University Press, 1967).

[5] *The Teaching of Jesus*, pp. 211-34.

[6] Tödt, *The Son of Man in the Synoptic Tradition* (Philadelphia: The Westminster Press, 1965); Higgins, *Jesus and the Son of Man* (Philadelphia: Fortress Press, 1965). Cf. now I. H. Marshall, "The Synoptic Son of Man Sayings in Recent Discussion," *New Testament Studies*, XII (1965-1966), 327-51.

other not less searching questions about them. In Mark 2, we have found that the son of man has power, *exousia*, to release a man from his sins and that he is lord, *kurios*, over the sabbath. Now, whatever else the son of man in Daniel 7 is, he is an exalted, righteous man (Dan. 7:13-14), possibly to be identified with the saints of the Most High (Dan. 7:22). Yet, he is still human; he is still even "humanity" in its perfect obedience to God. It is this Torah-righteous ideal man that Jesus claims himself to be, in deeds and in words, even though he overturns all previous notions of Torah-piety. It is this "man" that he claims "came not to be served but to serve, and to give his life as a ransom for many" (Mark 10:45). Whatever "son of man" is in its developed and complicated form in the Gospels, the term basically must mean "human being," "Adam," with the sense also that man-hood means Torah-righteousness (cf. Ps. 8:4; Ezek. 2:1), with the open-ended possibility that such a man can be "at God's right hand":

What is man, that thou art mindful of him,
    and the son of man that thou dost care for him? (Ps. 8:4)

Let thy hand be upon the man of thy right hand,
    the son of man whom thou hast made strong for thyself!
                                                    (Ps. 80:17.)

What, then, is the Hebrew expression *bar nashar* about? Basically, it is simply another way of saying "man," analogous to the psalmist's usage. If one wishes to go further and say that the expression as used in the Gospels cannot avoid having at least some titular significance, then we must say that the "son of man" is clearly something about humanity in its secular situation. But it is now in a new guise in the man Jesus, living "as if God were present" or, rather, *as if God were already in the secular*. It is about how this man Jesus can find acceptance specifically through a life of love, servanthood, self-denial, and suffering. And it may be also about the way any man gets to be "exalted to the right hand of God."

Third, we see Jesus here as the embodiment of a new Law and as beginning the task of relating this new Law to the requirements of the old. As soon as he began his work, the people noted that he taught "as one who had authority" (*exousia*, Mark 1:22)—not "with a note of authority," as NEB translates it.

There has been a long discussion in recent years of whether or not the Jews expected a "new" Torah prior to or at the messianic time or the Coming Age.[7] My own opinion is that, regardless of what was expected, it becomes clear that Jesus did in fact place himself "in the place of Torah," and that Torah here means not simply the "traditions of the elders" (which it certainly also does mean), but also the Old Testament, the Decalogue, and even on occasion the original will of God in creation (Mark 2:27-28). Jesus replaces all this with *himself*, the embodiment of the new Torah, analogous to wisdom embodying the old Torah. The Old Testament "follows the ways of God" in the old Torah. The New Testament "follows the ways of God" in Jesus, who is himself the new Torah. Jesus himself is the "new garment" the kingdom requires.[8]

Fourth, the actions and teaching of Jesus go hand in hand. This is not simply a device of the evangelist. Indeed, some of the more recent critics, far from doubting whether the juxtaposition of action and teaching brings suspicion upon a passage, feel that this very juxtaposition is a sign of probable

[7] Cf. W. D. Davies, *The Setting of the Sermon on the Mount*, pp. 433-35.

[8] Cf. Günther Bornkamm, *Jesus of Nazareth*, p. 96-109, who, however, does not see Jesus as a new Torah.

authenticity.[9] Whether that be so or not, we may see here that the teaching and works of Jesus are never separated. Indeed, already at Mark 1:27, the crowds have cried out, "What is this? A new teaching! With authority he commands even the unclean spirits, and they obey him." At that stage, Jesus has not spoken a word of teaching! It does not matter to Mark. It is the total impact of the words and deeds which have power, *exousia*.

So, here, in the debate about his actions in having table-fellowship with sinners, we have teaching about the purpose of his coming (Mark 2:17); in a discussion about his disciples' action in not fasting, we have teaching about the nature of the present crisis (Mark 2:19-22); and in answer to criticism about his disciples working on the sabbath, we have teaching on the new Law (Mark 2:27-28). The deeds have precipitated the questions, and the questions precipitate the teaching. The teaching stands under the actions, and the teaching and actions go hand in hand. The words which reveal himself are the words necessitated by the deeds.

And so on, throughout Mark's Gospel, goes the miserable procession of the demon-possessed, of the needy, or the misunderstanding, or mean, or confused, or hateful, or incomprehending; and so on, goes the procession of the deeds of God in Jesus for their salvation, which is healing, exorcism, reinstatement, manhood. Luke the physician's Gospel tells it all with even greater detail. He alone has the quotation from Isaiah (Isa. 61:1-2, 58:6) which forms the substance of Jesus' announcement of his mission when he preached in the synagogue at Nazareth (Mark 6:1-6):

[9] Cf. esp. Ernst Fuchs, *Studies in the Historical Jesus*, who associates this also with the speech-which-is-event (*Sprachereignis*) of preaching or cult. Similarly, Ernst Jüngel, *Paulus und Jesus* (Tübingen, 1962), pp. 273 ff., on speech-which-is-history (*Sprachgeschichte*).

The Spirit of the Lord is upon me,
because he has anointed me to preach good news to the poor.
He has sent me to proclaim release to the captives
and recovering of sight to the blind,
to set at liberty those who are oppressed,
to proclaim the acceptable year of the Lord. (Luke 4:18-19.)

Who finds acceptance with God, and how? Or, in the language that must perhaps be used if there are places (and there undoubtedly are) where the term "God" is meaningless, who finds acceptance in life? Who enters the fullness and meaning of human existence, who acknowledges by his deeds the presence already in the secular of the things which belong also to *shalom* (peace), the kingdom, the "accepted," the ultimate, the "transcendental"?

The answer of the New Testament is one and only one: "See Jesus, and you have it all—Father, heaven, way, truth, life." Look to Jesus, for he is the one who uniquely and representatively finds favor and acceptance. And what do I find when I look to Jesus? What does the Spirit-of-the-Lord-filled man do? Why, proclaims good news to poor people, lets out prisoners, gives sight to blind, and declares a day when men may find favor with God. How, again, do they find favor? By doing the deeds of the Spirit-filled Jesus, which are secular gospel for the hungry, secular gospel for prisoners, secular gospel for the blind.

Or look only at the deeds and then at the world's needs and Jesus healing them. Precisely whether a man sees this whole action of Jesus as messianic is the question whereby a man includes himself or excludes himself from acceptance.

But what is "acceptance"? How does a man involve himself in this whole Jesus-event? We turn to that in the next chapters. But first, we must examine the teaching of Jesus to which the deeds have now pointed us.

Chapter 9

PARABLES: THE HIDDENNESS OF THE KINGDOM

The teachings of Jesus usually receive scant attention from modern theologians. "Jesus was not just a great teacher," we are told in triumph. But the whole question needs to be opened up once more. In this chapter we shall concentrate our attention mainly on the parables, but it may help to fit this immediately into our total concern if we recall that the Gospels do not share our modern disinterest in what Jesus taught.

In the last chapter we saw that words were necessitated by actions. Conversely, the words precipitate healings and deeds. Jesus' "words" have peculiar and unique power. "The word" is what Jesus preaches (Mark 2:2) "with power" (Mark 1:22); it is the "word of God" (Luke 5:1). But this word "goes forth," is sown by the sower, and then takes upon itself a separate existence, and either bears fruit or is lost or stunted in its growth (Mark 4:3-20). Even without the detailed allegorical explanation of vss. 13-20, the seed could hardly be understood as anything other than the words of

Jesus. The word, once spoken, is thought of as enjoying a separate existence apart from the speaker. It comprises, indeed, a part of the speaker, which has passed over into and remains a part of the one who has "heard." Thus, the words have eschatological (Mark 8:38) and eternal (Mark 8:31) value. The words of Jesus have power (Luke 4:36; Matt. 8:8). Indeed, "the words" (*logoi*) can denote "the whole body of things said by Jesus" (Matt. 24:35; Mark 8:38), while *logos* can be used as a collective singular (Luke 10:39). The term "word" belongs especially to the person of Jesus. God was active in the words, just as he had been active in the word of creation: "Let there be" —and there was (Gen. 1). Just as the "Word became flesh" (John 1:1-4), so also the word "was" that which it became. It was action, movement, instruction, "dynamism." Carl Michalson, following J. L. Austin, uses the word "performatory" for it, and observes how "the word" in Christianity becomes also its own revelation:

The word not only effects a new situation. What it effects it simultaneously interprets. History since New Testament times is not events which are subsequently in need of interpretation. History is meaningful occurrence: events which confer meaning.[1]

Thus, the "word" is the whole Jesus-phenomenon which has to be described by the disciples, because *through* listening to it man becomes involved in everything which is of ultimate value.

That is what the parables are about, and we shall try to show that "history is meaningful occurrence, events which confer meaning." But first we must say something about the study of the parables over the past ten years.

[1] *The Rationality of Faith*, p. 146. Cf. Ernst Fuchs, *Religion in Geschichte und Gegenwart* (Tübingen, 1961), V, 434-40; Gerhard Kittel, *Theologisches Wörterbuch zum Neuen Testament*, IV (Stuttgart, 1942), 121-24.

Investigations into the theological meaning of the parables seem to have reached something of a stalemate. As far as background study is concerned, the careful categories of the form critics appear to have disappeared as it became gradually clearer that the Hebrew *māshāl* and the Aramaic *mathlā* could cover without embarrassment many more forms of parable-like units than classes could be found for. As far as interpretation is concerned, the stalemate seems to be largely because of three very common but highly questionable assumptions—that a parable must be "simple," that a parable cannot be an allegory, and that a parable must clarify rather than mystify.

Joachim Jeremias inherits from the liberals the common belief that Jesus was a comparatively simple teacher, could we only strip off later accretions and get back to his essential message. From the beginning of the church there was "an unconscious desire to discover a deeper meaning in the simple words of Jesus." [2] Why this is supposed to have been the case is never quite clear. That they should have been puzzled by many of the words—as we are—was to be expected. But that they should deliberately make what was already perplexing enough a matter more difficult is hard to believe.

More important, however, there does not seem to have ever been a time when the words were not perplexing. (1) That the disciples who first heard them found them so is plain from the logion Mark 4:10 ff., and the parable of the sower. We shall turn to these in a moment. (2) The claim of "simplicity" often misses the whole point of a parable or reduces it to banality. Dodd says that "in the parables of the Gospels . . . all is true to nature and to life," [3] and generally

[2] Joachim Jeremias, *The Parables of Jesus* (New York: Charles Scribner's Sons, 1955), p. 10.

[3] C. H. Dodd, *The Parables of the Kingdon* (Rev. ed.; New York: Charles Scribner's Sons, 1961), p. 20.

he feels happy in the presence of parables which are "natural and realistic." Unfortunately, this a priori preference tends to preclude the "element of surprise" which J. A. Findlay regards as the "essence of the parable." [4] The servant's debt to his lord of ten thousand talents in Matt. 18:23-25 is a wholly ridiculous amount and is designed by shock tactics to provoke thought at the wholly unnatural and unprecedented events and claims which are being described. Jülicher[5] was partly to blame for this concentration on a "single point and that a simple one." Certainly, his monumental work did much to clear the air in the study of the parables. But it left them almost exclusively in the hands of the kindly, untheological liberalism which even Dodd does not avoid—at least in parables which do not seem to have to do with the kingdom. Would Jesus have been at all concerned to make the kind of banal moralisms which our frequent interpretations of the parables attribute to him? (3) It should never be forgotten that the Semitic mind took great pleasure in drama and exaggeration in the presentation of a truth. "Greater importance attaches to the words of scribes than to those of Torah" (*Sanhedrin* 11.3) did not mean exactly what it says. Anton Fridrichsen has pointed out that Jesus used prefatory illustrations which gave little indication of the final comment but to indicate its radical nature. So there is no connection between the illustration of the reed and the character of John the Baptist, any more than the illustration of the lion roaring in the forest conveys more than very remotely the idea of the coming destruction (Amos 3:4-8).[6] Such use of hyperbole, again, should make us suspicious of attempts to make the parables too simple.

---

[4] *Jesus and His Parables* (Naperville, Ill.: Alec R. Allenson, 1957), p. 10.

[5] Adolf Jülicher, *Die Gleichnisreden Jesu* (Tübingen, 1888-89).

[6] "La Priamèle dans l'enseignement de Jésus" in *Coniectanea Neotestamentica*, IV (Lund, 1940), 9-16.

The presupposition that the parables were intended to convey a simple message also probably lies behind the widespread suspicion of "allegory" in the parables. Jülicher sufficiently showed the havoc which allegory can play. But within the rabbinical tradition, what Dibelius calls "half-allegorical forms" are found repeatedly, such as the representation of God by a king, the people by a vineyard, the world by a field, the last judgment by a harvest, the beginning of the messianic era by a marriage.[7] Whenever these words were used, the necessary identification was made in the mind automatically. Every case must be judged upon its own merits. All that we can observe at the outset is the predisposition of the Semitic mind to make identifications and then to stick to them.

The important decision to be made with each parable, therefore, as Max Meinertz has said, is to discover "what is not immediately certain—how great a role allegory plays." [8] We may say immediately that the allegorical explanations which the Gospels already supply—those of the sower (Mark 4:13-20) and of the tares (Matt. 13:36-43)—are in their present form secondary. Indeed, we might add, the very singularity of such forced interpretations suggests that the normal method of allegorical realization—or "seeing the point" of the parables—has been abandoned in these two cases. Again, God is not the man dragged from his bed by a late caller's persistency (Luke 11:5-8) or the judge who settles a case just to get a bit of peace from a nagging complainant (Luke 18:1-8). On the other hand, it would be difficult to make any kind of sense at all, were it not to be taken that God is represented by the father who gives gifts

[7] Martin Dibelius, *From Tradition to Gospel* (New York: Charles Scribner's Sons, 1965), p. 255.

[8] "Zum Verständnis der Gleichnisse Jesu" in *Das Heilige Land*, LXXXVI (1954), pp. 41-47.

to his child (Matt. 7:9-11), the father rejoicing at the return of the prodigal (Luke 15:11-32), the one who forgives the penitent publican (Luke 18:9-14), or the one who rewards equally (Matt. 20:1-16) or according to merit (Matt. 25: 14-30). Now, all these must be called more or less allegorical. In each case, God and man or a man are represented, and a third factor as well.

The real danger in the hunt-the-allegory type of parable interpretation is that we shall miss the basic purpose of parables in the activity of our Lord. Rudolf Bultmann distinguishes between the "point" and the "(allegorical) application" of a parable.[9] This basic purpose or "point" I take to be not instruction or apologetics or controversy, but concealed revelation about life (the kingdom), and concealed revelation about himself (Christology). That is to say, the main aim of the parables is to describe the activity of God in Jesus, more particularly so that men may trust in it and become disciples, or else be offended at it. The parables are evidence of Jesus' "evangelistic strategy."

The parable at once deepens the understanding of those who already follow and also arouses decision in those who merely listen. That this was, in fact, the reason why Jesus used parables accords well with the nature of the Jewish parable, which lies between parable and allegory, and poses a picture or problem for the hearers to discern or answer. Oriental storytelling, says Dibelius, lies close to the riddle (*Rätsel*).[10] The allegorical interpretations already in the Gospels are not riddles; they are dull morals drawn by the church. But the allegorical interpretations latent there are riddles.

[9] *History of the Synoptic Tradition* (New York: Harper & Row, 1963), pp. 193-222.

[10] *From Tradition to Gospel*, p. 256. Paul Fiebig, *Die Gleichnisreden Jesu* (Tübingen, 1912), pp. 253-67, puts most of Jesus' parables in this class "between parable and allegory."

The problematical text (Mark 4:10 ff.), with its claim that Jesus told parables so that outsiders "seeing might not see," cannot be regarded as an adequate statement of the aim of the parabolic teaching; apart from anything else, it implies that parable teaching was solely for outsiders (vs. 11). But the verses do describe the actual results of the parables, for people did see the story but not the point of the story. Parables, then, as Austin Farrar shows,[11] both hide and reveal; they come "riddlingly to those without," for "we cannot understand the analogy of a mysterious thing to a plain thing without some grasp of the mysterious thing." The revelation must be paradoxical and mysterious because to understand means to commit oneself to the one who is revealed. "Whether one believes," says Ernst Fuchs, "—on that hangs also whether one comes into mutual understanding with Him." [12]

What then is the "riddle" hidden within the parables?

One difficulty with the parables is that we usually think of them as illustrations rather than riddles. We say that Jesus used homely illustrations to convey profound truths, and so on. What he seems to have done, however, is to have told stories about real or fantastic situations in order to pose questions to people, which they would worry over, and then—perhaps—see the point.

Thus, it probably does not matter whether a parable begins "the kingdom of heaven (or God) is like . . ." or whether it begins "consider . . ." or "look at . . ."; the purpose is the same. And this purpose is not, I suggest, simply to *use*

[11] *A Study in St. Mark* (Naperville, Ill.: Alec R. Allenson, 1951), pp. 241-42. On Mark 4:10 ff., cf. William Manson, *Expository Times*, LXVIII (1957), 132-35; T. A. Burkhill, *Mysterious Revelation* (Ithaca, N. Y.: Cornell University Press, 1963).

[12] *Hermeneutik* (Bad Cannstatt, 1954), p. 229.

secular or worldly or human illustrations in order to get over a truth (which is what the Gospel writers make of many of them). Rather it is to direct people into their own experience to see the true significance even of the secular events themselves, now that the open possibility of the kingdom stands before them.

Is this the "riddle"? Let us see how far the parabolic material comes alive in this way.

(1) *The parables indicate the way in which, quite unconsciously, men have been dealing with the issues of the kingdom within the secular.*

The entire point of a number of the parables is to indicate how persons engaged in ordinary secular activities have, in fact, been dealing with the ultimately significant issues—the issues of the mysteriously present kingdom, the issues tied up with Jesus as the Messiah, the issues relating to their salvation. The laborers who come at the eleventh hour (Matt. 20:1-15) do not know that in fact the Lord is going to choose to treat them as he treats the rest, who have borne the heat and burden of the day. They did more than they knew when they came in at that ridiculous hour. The tiny grain of mustard seed (Matt. 13:31-32) does not know that it simply has to remain "in itself," growing as naturally as it can, so that in the end it will be as big as a tree and birds will come and make nests in its branches. The good Samaritan (Luke 10:25-37) does not know that he is going to fulfill the one thing needful—to know what in fact and in deed to be a neighbor really means. The servant who faithfully trades with the pound which his master has lent him (Luke 19:11-26) does not know that that will entitle him to be given even more of his master's work for which to be responsible. The man who is like the tares does not imagine, while he gaily grows alongside the wheat and thinks himself every bit as good as it, that the harvest will come and he will be cast into the rubbish heap to be burned (Matt. 13:24-30). The Pharisee and the publican do not know who goes "down to his house justified" (Luke 18:9-14). And so on.

The riddle in all this is really very plain and really very complicated—which accounts for Mark's theory about parables. The plain matter is that "the kingdom of heaven is like" what life is like—having the nous to see in ordinary or extraordinary events the real thing which is important. Go on, says Jesus, worry at it until you see if your life has to be different because of this new way of carrying on the business of living! It's near enough to you!

(2) *The secular is the sphere which passively conceals the significance of the events going on within it.*

Throughout the Gospels, the world (*kosmos*), seems to be merely the neutral background for the drama.[13] Thus, in the parables the world is the field, possessing both good and bad ground and various kinds of each, into which the sower sows his seed (Mark 4:3-20). All the nature parables, especially the parables of growth, depend for their point upon the existence of a completely neutral and constant earthly background (e.g. the mustard seed, Mark 4:30-32; the leaven, Matt. 13:33). Goodness or badness belongs to the human participants in the parables, certainly not to the world as a physical entity. Indeed, the parables of growth and that of the patient husbandman (Mark 4:26-29) suggest that the earth can well care for its charges if it is left to work in its own way. The tares among the wheat (Matt. 13:24-30) in any case must be left until the harvest, when it will be made clear what is of value and what is useless. The "acted parable"

[13] Cf. George Johnston, "*Oikoumene* and *kosmos* in the New Testament," *New Testament Studies*, X (1964), 352-60.

of the cursed fig tree (Luke 13:6-9) does not alter this essentially neutral character of the created order.

(3) *Obedience consists in a right use of the secular.*

The "stewardship" parables make this plain. Frequently, the whole point of a parable is that one of the actors is praised for a good deed. "The Lord commends" not only the "unjust steward" (Luke 16:1-8), but also the faithful servant (Luke 17:7-10), those who use the talents rightly (Matt. 25:14-30), and many others whose actions illustrate some aspect of the work of Christ. Indeed, the children of the world are in their generation wiser than the children of light (Luke 16:8), for they understand what is expected of man as God's "steward."

The world is, admittedly, the area of the kind of anxious care for the morrow which is denied the disciple (Matt. 6:34); "the cares of the world and the delight in riches" choke the word of the gospel (Matt. 13:22); the money buried in "the world" will mean a heart buried there also (Matt. 6:21). But there is nothing inherent in the world or in man's worldly condition or status which demands that this must be so, or that man is powerless to make it different. Indeed, the whole point of the parabolic method is that man is able to make the decisions demanded of him and in particular to decide whether he will serve God or mammon.

But, if he decides to serve God, his service will not be in an area or in terms different from that in which he would have served mammon. The world, and presumably mankind within it, remains the neutral scene on which are played the dramas of personal decision in every man's life. The beatitudes of Luke 6:20-26 make this abundantly clear. Nothing could possibly be more down-to-earth than this kind of blessedness. The blessings pronounced seem to depend entirely upon worldly conditions. Matthew was obviously acutely conscious of the problem involved!

(4) *Man's response to the parables is his response to the hidden kingdom.*

The kingdom is thus hidden within the world. Thus, the disciple belongs as much to the world as the "worldly" opposer does. Whether in fact the world can ever be the scene of the kingdom of God is left open. But if the kingdom means "God's rule being obeyed," rather than "a geographical area of obedience," then we may say that the kingdom is "of this world," since the only place in which the individual may obey God's commands is within the concrete life of this world.

The whole good news of the Gospels is utterly realistic, secular. God has a world which he requires to be run his way. The way is shown to us in Jesus, the acceptable steward, who does what no one before him did in carrying out the behest of his master, God. Now the Christian disciple is the steward, responsible through Christ to God for the universe.

The parables, then, were intended to do more in the intention of Jesus than they at present do in the Gospels. As Jeremias has shown, the things they do now in the Gospels are not necessarily the things they might have been expected to do in the purpose of Jesus. But behind every parable lie two simple truths. First, there stands now in this moment of time, before everyone who hears, the one in whom are all the secrets of life, who is indeed hidden in some way in every parable (even if this can be overdone[14]). And second, there lies the complementary truth—that a man must wrestle with

---

[14] Cf. my paper, "The Parables of Jesus as Self-Revelation," *Studia Evangelica* (Berlin, 1959), pp. 84-109. The earlier pages are summarized at the beginning of this chapter.

this particular story of the parable to see how already in his secular existence he might have had to deal with the ultimately significant, the issue of his salvation. Has he already said Yes but not done his father's will (Matt. 21:30)? Has he been blind to the real issues at stake in some situation where he mistakenly thought he had only himself and his barns to consider (Luke 12:16-21)?

Basically, then, the kingdom of God in the Gospels represents not simply Jesus' deeds but also whatever can be said to partake in or be like Jesus' deeds, and hence to have value before God—to have ultimate, final, or transcendental value. But so far as human beings are concerned, this ultimate, final, or transcendental is to be encountered exclusively in the secular. This, indeed, is the whole point of the "coming" of Jesus—to bring that which has ultimate significance—the kingdom of God—into immediate proximity to man.

And man must make his response to the hidden kingdom "by faith"—that is, without seeing whether the ultimate, final, or transcendental in fact are involved. I have only used these words at all because they amplify in contemporary jargon the notion of the kingdom. But none of them is basic or necessary. For the kingdom is not something exterior to the secular, added to it from above or outside it. The kingdom is genuinely *within* the secular, *part* of it, *met* within it.

(5) *Man's response to the hidden kingdom is the issue of love to neighbor.*

There are two ways in which a man has to deal with the kingdom. Either he has "got" the kingdom because he has been grasped by Jesus in healing or mercy (ch. 8), or else he has been involved in its issues already in his life and relationships (this chapter). But this also means that he has been dealing with the issue of "neighborliness," as becomes clear in the parable of the good Samaritan.

119

The lawyer's question, "What shall I do to inherit eternal life?" (Luke 10:25), which is the question everybody is supposed to be asking the church (though it is a long time since I have heard it), is answered by Jesus in a perfectly practical way: Fulfill the typical summary requirements of Torah regarding love of God and neighbor. "Do that and you will live," says Jesus. The man persisting with the question, "Who is my neighbor?" gets no answer. There is no answer to this question. The only thing that Jesus says in reply is that the only person who is entitled to say who is a neighbor is the man lying on the roadside (vs. 36). The story claims that there is no answer to the human problem of existence in a man trying to sort out his own position in life. "How can I be a decent Christian?" "Who is my neighbor, so that I can get on with the job?" we ask. Jesus does not answer the questions. What he does do is to tell the story about this wretched man lying on the roadside. And then he says that the only possibility of talking about neighbors rests in the man who needs a neighbor.

And is not Jesus profoundly right, even in our own experience? You can never go to somebody and say, "I will love this man because he is my neighbor," or "I will be a good neighbor to him." The only person entitled to say whether neighborliness exists is the man on the roadside. And once again what Jesus has done is to remove the commandment from the possibility of fulfillment. Luther and Calvin and the great theologians of the Reformation used to use this as an illustration of the fact that you cannot do anything about the gospel until you have been saved by grace. But what Jesus actually did was to remove the command from the possibility of fulfillment because it is not given to mankind to deal directly with God or God's acceptance. The issues of the kingdom—and they are all tied up with finding the neighbor—can only be dealt with indirectly. The command is no longer within the realm of calculated, intentional fulfillment. Eternal life remains a far-off possibility, dependent on this man on the roadside finding a neighbor!

The dialogue with the ruler (Luke 18:18-23; Mark 10:17-22; Matt. 19:16-22), in answer to the same question about eternal life, is strictly parallel. In this case, Jesus himself claims to be the one who makes the demand for love. In this case he tells the ruler to give to the poor and follow him. Here, the claimant is clarified. It is Jesus. And what is being said here is that all situations in which man is confronted by the need to be a neighbor are Jesus-situations. But the Jesus-situations are hidden within that which we could normally consider to be merely secular incidents.

(6) *"Love to neighbor"* is the issue of judgment.

Our "hidden secrets of the kingdom" is carried to its final stage—though it is implied by all that we have already said—in Matt. 25:35-45, with the parable of the sheep and the goats. This is essentially a parable about how the non-disciples will be judged by the way in which they have unintentionally responded to the actual but hidden presence of Christ in the person of needy, homeless, sick, or imprisoned people.[15] The church members who have been on the lookout for Christ are in agony when they discover that their failure to discern in the needy the presence of the issue of their salvation was because they failed to see in the needy the presence of Christ. The parable bristles with scholarly problems, but its point is plain. Christ is already present in the secular deed, perhaps every secular deed, when a man's only thought is to respond authentically and generously to what is asked of him in the confronting situation. As Chrysostom has it, "You have seen your brother? You have seen your Lord."

It is a mistake to imagine that Matthew 25 is in any way

---

[15] Cf. Jeremias, *The Parables of Jesus*, p. 209.

peculiar in its teaching. Paul seems to have been happy that self-interested and schismatic people yet preached Christ (Phil. 1:6). We shall see the same thing even more in Colossians.

All this must be stretched to its limit in the modern secular search for a "Christian God."

No-one can come to God except through his neighbour and through his neighbour's child. We worship God when we worship the ultimate mystery and uniqueness of our fellow man. When we betray a man, we commit an ultimate act of apostasy; we choose an inhuman God.[16]

It is grace that I can see Christ in my neighbor (Bonhoeffer). The question is: But Lord, when did we see you? John Robinson may be right in believing that modern man is not looking for any kind of Messiah and that this son of man *incognito,* this Christ as the gracious neighbor, this man for others and with others, may be the one who may become known ultimately to modern man as Messiah.[17] Thus, there is a superficial sense in which Hugh Montefiore was right to criticize Robinson's chapter heading and Erik Routley's book title, "The Man for Others," and insist that the better title for the Jesus of the Gospels was "The Man for God." [18] Unless, of course, as the evidence suggests, to be "for others" is the only possible worldly, secular form of being "for God," and unless we probe further into the Christology of the New Testament to ask whether or not the Lord has a relation to the ultimate which the disciple now has not directly with God, but mediately through the Lord Jesus.

[16] Werner Pelz, *The Listener,* December 28, 1961.

[17] Robinson, *The New Reformation?* pp. 35 ff.

[18] Montefiore, *Frontier,* Spring, 1965, pp. 68-69.

Much of the teaching ministry of Jesus seems to have been occupied with what we today would call "nonreligious discourse." This is because the Gospel writers believe that the purpose of Jesus' coming was to declare the presence of the ultimately significant, first in Jesus' deeds and, secondly, in every deed in the way illuminated by Jesus.

As his conduct shows, Jesus clearly did not want to be understood apart from his proclamation, but rather in it. His whole proclamation is one single self-testimony, not as witness for his possible messianic consciousness (for in my opinion Jesus spoke definitely only of the future Son of Man), but because this proclamation presupposes a new being of man, in which God speaks with the individual; and as a result, the individual also is able to speak freely of God, as the parables of the labourers in the vineyard and the prodigal son do. . . . Jesus did not claim for himself a special position before God. He understood himself as *the witness of a new situation,* as the authentic witness for the exposition of the future of the rule of God; an exposition which is valid now in his own presence.[19]

But what is the new situation? It is that the whole world-affirming, concrete, mundane way of Torah is now indeed "fulfilled" in a way that is exactly as world-affirming, concrete, and mundane, except that now this way is *hidden,* hidden within a man's response to the human Jesus who stands before him and to the issues of existence to which he points.

There is, then, a secular Christ. But the secular Christ exists in his own right and not merely because modern man thinks he seeks him. There is a secular Christ, but this is not at all the kind of Christ that modern secular man maps out for himself when he seeks to create a Christ after his own image. There are points in the Synoptic story which shout at us in our contemporary search. But we must still allow the Gospel to tell its own story in its own way.

[19] Ernst Fuchs, *Studies of the Historical Jesus,* p. 224.

And the Synoptic Gospels tell a thoroughly "secular" story, that is, a story about a man in this world who stands as the one who is anointed by God. His work of both teaching and healing compels avowal of his uniqueness. His actions in purely secular situations, such as eating or healing, calling or speaking, as such betoken in his view, or in the view of the evangelists the corresponding actions of God. The parables declare the hidden presence of the kingdom already within apparently artless secular deeds. Everything pertaining to God—his forgiveness, his prerogative of mercy and judgment—is brought down to earth, down to the secular. Now, the only way to encounter God is to take with utter seriousness, generosity, and joy the man before me, be it Christ or my neighbor (who dare tell one from the other?). Only so can there be any dealing with the ultimate, the significant, the kingdom; and only through them can man, with necessary hesitation and humor, presume to think that he has dealt with God.

Jesus strictly represents the secularization of God. All of God that can be encountered by man is to be encountered in the man Jesus, in his deeds, and in his words that describe deeds. The question facing every man is: Do you dare to show by a deed that it could be true?

The "ultimate" must be dealt with entirely in the "penultimate," for that is the place where God in Jesus is.[20]

And all this is *gospel*, good news. It is *gospel* that the ultimately acceptable lies hidden within the deeds of the world. It is *gospel* that every man, be he believer or atheist, disciple or opposer, in fact can minister secretly, whether he wills or not, to the same fundamental redeeming purposes within creation. Thus, man can go into his world with

[20] Cf. Bonhoeffer, *Ethics* (New York: Macmillan Paperbacks, 1965), pp. 125-26; Dietrich von Oppen, *Das personale Zeitalter* (Stuttgart: Horley Verlag, 1960).

hilaritas, with gaiety, with confidence, with assurance. For God is in the midst of it. Thus man can go into every relationship which seems to him to have "value," in which he shows love, mercy, laughter, pity, or tears, knowing that ultimately the things he finds there are not mockeries of reality, but the real thing, the real God, the real presence. If he be a believer, a Christian, he might, with necessary humor, self-effacement, and embarrassment, point to the significant and the redemptive, as he has seen Jesus point. But he goes, in any case, in confidence and abandon, knowing that God will have the last laugh, but that the last laugh does not mock what has seemed already to be the robe of Jesus along the way.

Chapter 10

DISCIPLESHIP: THE FAITH THAT WORKS

In this chapter we inquire further into the human response to Jesus, the response described in those who are healed or forgiven as "faith," in those who are called to follow as "discipleship," and in those who are compelled to change their whole way of life as "repentance." We take the last group first.

(1) *The response to Jesus can only be in deeds.*

Jesus sits and eats with the Pharisees. The living Torah, God's very presence, is with them. Jesus sits and eats with the publicans and sinners. The living Torah, God's very presence, is with them also. The Pharisee yet fails to have part in him because of hardness of heart and unwillingness to leave the old and love the radically new. How may the publicans and sinners participate in him, the one who comes to them whether they invite him or not, understand him or not, receive him or not? Basically they must participate in him in the same way as the disciples may participate in him:

by the deeds in which his deeds are discovered—the deeds of mercy, healing, and forgiveness. These are the deeds of the publicans and harlots who go into heaven before the scribes and Pharisees (Matt. 21:31). For the publican, seeing Jesus, has him to tea and through this encounter gives away all his ill-gotten gain (Luke 19:1-10). The sinner, seeing Jesus, bathes his feet as if she were hostess and has her sins forgiven (Luke 7:37-50). And joy breaks out in heaven! (Luke 15:7.)

The good news of Jesus is that now, because of him and in him, God is hidden within the secular. Now, to be obedient to God is to live in the light of God's presence in the man Jesus within secular situations and relationships. This is essentially what Jesus is talking about when he promises the disciples that "whoever would save his life will lose it; and whoever loses his life for my sake . . . will save it" (Mark 8: 35). He who attempts to deal directly with the kingdom will be thwarted. Man can only deal with the kingdom indirectly, through concrete obedience to Jesus, through responding to the hidden presence of the Jesus-issue, the kingdom, in ordinary everyday decisions.

The only time the Gospel writers use the word "salvation" is in this connection. "Today salvation has come to this house" (Luke 19:9) is Jesus' comment upon Zacchaeus' generosity. How had the salvation come? By a man seeing in Jesus eating with him at his home, the present possibility of acceptance and forgiveness, represented by the prophet-righteous man who has come to the house. How did salvation come? By Zacchaeus seeing in the presence of Jesus the demand for self-sacrifice to the poor and repayment four times over to those defrauded. This is salvation—secular self-sacrifice, secular reinstatement, secular compensation. The only way in which man may know salvation is in his secular discipleship. Jesus has come to tell Zacchaeus—and all of us—precisely this.

Is there then no breaking of the inexorable law of consequences? Can we never get away from the judgment of our dealing with the hidden Christ in the secular? One thing breaks this inexorable law: *forgiveness*. But how does a man come by forgiveness? By beseeching the gates of heaven for a revocation of the consequences already set in train by his dealing with the hidden Christ? Indeed no. The plea, "forgive us our trespasses," can only be made by one who is actively forgiving those trespassing against him (Matt. 6:12; Luke 11:4). The whole transaction is perfectly straightforward and automatic. No divine act is required or assumed. "If you forgive men their trespasses, your heavenly Father also will forgive you; but if you do not forgive men their trespasses, neither will your Father forgive your trespasses." (Matt. 6:14-15.) As Mark 11:25 has it, "whenever you stand praying, forgive, if you have anything against any one; so that [*hina kai*] your Father also who is in heaven may forgive you your trespasses." The man who does not forgive the trifle his brother owes him will find himself in jail with the utterly impossible task of paying what he owes to God (Matt. 18:21-35).

Here again, the only way out that admits a man to the kingdom is a man's secular deed. This, precisely, is the "good news." God is actually, unbelievably willing to forgive men their transgressions against his holy and spotless Torah, his Law. How can men receive this priceless gift? By repenting (*metanoia*). And repenting means being prepared to see divine forgiveness as hanging upon human forgiveness. This is the great difference between repentance for Jesus and repentance for John the Baptist or the prophets. Repentance for Jesus is "hidden" within what a man does in response to the demands over against him.

This is what is meant by repenting, by being converted (*metanoia*). Repentance as a genuine turning round cannot simply mean "believing in Jesus." Rather it means believing in the new fact of the kingdom represented by Jesus. Thus, Jesus' call to penitence is to be understood as a call to love, which, as we have seen, is simply and complicatedly living existence in the light of Jesus' presence—simply obedience to God through one's neighbor. As Bultmann says, "In the demand for obedience, the old man escapes from himself (self-love)" and comes "under God's lordship—either the lordship of a jealous God of judgment or that of the God of compassion." He then becomes either a sinner or a justified man.[1] Fuchs has asked whether there is any difference between this and "purposely calculated righteousness by works." (Cf. James 2:21-26.)

When I really submit to a commandment, in the sense that I begin to live for my neighbour irrespective of all feeling of sympathy, then the question of myself no longer interests me; nor am I interested in the question of the characteristic of my conduct, namely obedience. What does concern me is the concrete question of what I can do for my neighbour and what not.[2]

Those who love are relieved of judgment (Matt. 5:27 ff). Man must love in view of the *present* action of God in Jesus, not in view of eschatological judgment. All man can do is "be found." Fuchs says it is "not a word or deed, but an event that happens to me."[3] The parables are about God's demanding man's "nonaction" and, therefore, his *discovery*.

Thus, Jesus does not ignore or reduce the value of the good. Because the father loves the prodigal, he does not love the elder brother any less (Luke 15:31). The fact that the

[1] Rudolf Bultmann, *Jesus* (Wiedenfeld and Nicholson, 1930), p. 93.
[2] Ernst Fuchs, *Studies of the Historical Jesus*, p. 119.
[3] *Ibid.*, p. 130.

publican is humble and realistic does not mean that God prefers his life to the Torah-obedient life of the Pharisee (Luke 18:10-14). Jesus, seeing the young man who had kept the commandments, "loved him" (Mark 10:17 ff.). There is no lessening of God's concern with righteousness.

Rather, there is a "sharpening" of righteousness, and a reduction or specifying of righteousness. In the first place, there is a sharpening. Such a sharpening of Torah was expected in some of the rabbinical writings as a prelude to the coming of the Messiah. Qumran represents precisely this. There are radical elements in Jesus' demand, especially in the demands for avoiding sin "in the heart," contained in the radical reinterpretations of the Old Testament Law. Jesus' complaints against the human traditions of the Pharisees were not that they made things too hard for people, but that their rules set aside the higher rules (e.g., *korban,* setting aside commandments to honor parents, Mark 7:8-13). The disciples' righteousness must *exceed* that of the Pharisees (Matt. 5:20).[4]

The other element—the reduction or specifying of the demands of God—is a logical development of the first. The total requirement of God can clearly not be met in this life. Hence, says Albert Schweitzer, it belongs exclusively to the future. But another suggestion has recently been put forward by Krister Stendhal—that the strict demands of God are due to "messianic license." [5] He begins by observing how Matt. 19:10-12 cancels a law even of creation (Gen. 1:28) by saying that there can be people excused the marriage commanded by the Law "for the sake of the kingdom of heaven." Similarly, Paul in I Cor. 7:25-40 argues that a man

[4] Cf. Herbert Braun, *Spätjüdisch-häretischer und frühchristlicher Radikalismus* (Tübingen, 1957), I and II.

[5] "Messianic License" in *Biblical Realism Confronts the Nation,* ed. Paul Peachey (Nyack, N. Y.: Fellowship Publications, 1963), pp. 139-52.

would be justified in breaking an engagement to marry because of the eschatological situation. Thus, the disciple today may (not must) act on the basis of the "messianic license," but he must realize that it is "subversive" and that the disciples may have to pay the price of such action.

What can the underlying purpose here be? Is it not that Paul and Matthew understand that Jesus always taught that sometimes the standards of goodness could only be obeyed by so radically stepping outside them that they were brought into question in relation to the kingdom of God? Is this not exactly the purpose of Jesus' challenge to the young man (Mark 10:20-22) which brings forth the amazed, "Then who can be saved?" (vs. 26).

(2) *Faith: Involvement in God's action.*

Faith in the Gospels is always "preparedness to do something, or have something done to you." Faith is that by which healing takes place (Mark 5:34, 10:52). If you have faith, you can be healed (Luke 18:42). Your faith "saves" you (Luke 8:25). If you had faith, you could move this mountain (Mark 11:23). If you had faith, you could walk on the water (to Peter, Matt. 14:28-31). Have faith in God (Mark 11:22). But faith is lacking in Israel (cf. Luke 7:9). Apart from the cases of the healing miracles, the "faith" in fact is not forthcoming. Faith is what the disciples lack (Mark 9:14-29); (cf. "prayer and fasting" in vs. 29). How is it that you have no faith? (Mark 4:40). Lord, "increase our faith," the disciples pray (Luke 17:5). But, in the end, faith will not be found on earth, even when the son of man comes (Luke 18:8).

In the case of the healing miracles which succeed, it seems that "faith" constituted the supreme effort by the recipient to grasp the proffered healing of Christ. Thus Mark 2:5: "When Jesus saw their faith [of the men lowering him through the roof], he said to the paralytic, 'My son, your sins are forgiven.' "

Instructive in this connection is Mark's addition of "this kind cannot be driven out by anything but prayer [and fasting]" at Mark 9:29 in a story in which the disciples' lack of faith (vss. 19, 23) had been the cause of their inability to cure a demoniac boy. Clearly, Mark (or Jesus) regards prayer (and fasting) as part of, if not synonymous with, faith. Sometimes "faith" is not mentioned, just the *action*: "Stretch out your hand," Jesus tells the man with the withered arm (Mark 3:5), and healing followed. "As many as touched [him] were healed," records Mark 6:56. The woman who touched his garment has the issue of blood dried up (Mark 5:28 ff.), and it is Jesus who gives this action the description "faith" (vs. 34). Matthew systematizes the matter of faith more than Mark, although even there the confusion and interrelatedness between faith and action are not wholly lost; what is new, though, is that faith is ecclesiastically oriented.[6]

What is faith, then? Basically, it is preparedness to launch myself unreservedly upon the unprovable assumption that God stands behind this Jesus. In the presence of Jesus, faith means simply the preparedness to act on the unprovable, the unprovable which can only possibly be accredited by my willingness to act. Faith is the preparedness to operate as if the unprovable—the presence of God within Jesus of Nazareth, the presence of the ultimate within the secular—were demonstrable. Faith is the preparedness to take a step over the cliff—perhaps underneath are the everlasting arms! Faith is the walking on water—which no man can do. As Kierkegaard says, faith *is* "walking on 70,000 fathoms of water."

"But I cannot walk on one inch of water," I retort.

* Cf. Günther Bornkamm, "End-Expectation and Church in Matthew" in *Tradition and Interpretation in Matthew* (Philadelphia: The Westminster Press, 1963), pp. 15-50.

132

Precisely. No more than I can have "faith." I cannot move mountains, or fig trees (Matt. 21:21), or even heal the sick (Mark 9:18). Just a tiny bit would do! (Matt. 17:20.)

Faith is absent in the Gospels in every case except those in which a person has faith to be healed. Indeed, this absence of faith is even more instructive than its presence. The early church reflected in the Gospels was *not* characterized by faith. Faith was from the beginning the ability to move mountains, walk on the water, heal the sick, and so forth. It was always the "impossible possibility." Faith was always hyperbolic, always outside the willingness to do the impossible. Yet it was also always linked with the person and work of Jesus, the "new fact" within the worldly order that made "faith" the only possible reply.

Indeed, faith in any serious sense only comes into the situation where all proof is absent—in the centurion seeing Jesus cry, "My God, my God, why hast thou forsaken me?" and declaring, "Truly this man was a son of God" (Mark 15:39). As Eduard Schweizer has put it, "Recognition of God in earnest begins with the recognition of the hidden God." [7]

Do not the miracles represent, nevertheless, some kind of demonstration, if not "proof," in the light of which faith becomes possible, particularly if in fact the only places where faith is found in the Gospels are the places where faith is a prelude to healing? No. For faith is not always found, even in connection with miracles. And the decisive thing about miracles is the wonderworking power or *exousia*, which appears like a dynamic force wherever man can lay hold on it. But the fact of the healings by Jesus never removes the arbitrariness of the event, which is truly momentary and dynamistic. Ultimately, the miracles do not break the incog-

[7] "Mark's Contribution to the Quest of the Historical Jesus," *New Testament Studies*, X (1963–1964), 421-32.

nito. They do not constitute any compelling claim. Miracles, among the religions of the ancient world, were widespread and seem to have been as well attested as in the case of Jesus. They belong, essentially, to the world of human effort to secure the extraordinary, the world of magic. Precisely this is the objection to Jesus—that he performs his miracles "by Beelzebub" (Mark 3:22; Luke 11:15; Matt. 12:24). And the answer of Jesus is just as instructive, if we follow Luke and Matthew: "By whom do your sons cast them out?" (Luke 11:19; Matt. 12:27). If there is a power of miracle given to men, it is either wholly of God or wholly of the devil, regardless of who is the operator, be it the disciples of the Pharisees, or people who use the name of Jesus, or Jesus himself. But power to work miracles certainly has nothing to do with the uniqueness of Jesus, which Jesus here explicitly confirms by accepting and asserting that others have the same power.

In fact, as Jesus constantly observed, miracles do not provide a stimulus to genuine belief. "Neither will they be convinced if some one should rise from the dead" (Luke 16: 31). In the presence of Jesus, faith means simply preparedness to act on the unprovable which can only possibly be accredited by my acting. This is why Jesus asks if people have "faith to be healed," why he emphasizes the importance of faith to healing. Within the Christian community, this willingness to have miracles wrought on one is the function of faith. But it can never be reduced to "believing in miracles."

Belief in miracles is belief in a visible epiphany. Nothing happens in me if I assert my belief in miracles. There is only faith where a man so surrenders himself to the humiliated God-man as to stake his life on him, even when this seems against all sense.[8]

[8] Bonhoeffer, *Christ the Center,* pp. 114-15. R. H. Fuller, *Interpreting the Miracles* (Philadelphia: The Westminster Press, 1963), pp. 42-45, takes only a slightly different view.

What, then, are we to say about faith? With the exception of the faith of those who are to be healed, faith is rather a washout in the Gospels. The main reason for this seems to be that faith in a *simple* sense is fairly easy—believing in the facts connected with Jesus (as in Acts and Paul?). But faith in any serious sense is almost impossible—possible only with God.

How does this relate to some current theological positions? Faith has become, with the existentialists, "an interior act of the will," in line with the Reformation preaching of justification by faith alone. It becomes with Paul van Buren the "blik," the view of history which determines my attitude to life. With John Robinson and Tillich it becomes my sense of an already existing "depth." Paul van Buren describes this faith, first in Jesus and then in the disciple, as freedom. According to van Buren, Jesus' faith was "his genuine, personal, autonomous existence," so that the secular meaning of "faith in God" is "freedom to act humanly, without anxiety." [9] But is the word "freedom" being correctly used? Rather, I would speak of "willingness to act on the unprovable," with the emphasis as it is in the Gospels on the specific deed of action and not the intellectual discussion afterward of what proof or explanation is to be offered.

However, this may, of course, be a long way from Protestant theology. What can "faith" be? Bultmann says:

Pistis ["faith"] is understood as the acceptance of the Christian kerygma and therefore as *saving faith* which in acknowledging the work of God, accomplished in Christ, makes it his own. Naturally, *pistis* contains here also the sense of faith as a giving of credentials and in addition the elements of obedience, trust, hope and steadfastness might be connoted—just as, vice versa, where one

[9] *The Secular Meaning of the Gospel* (New York: The Macmillan Company, 1963), pp. 123 ff.

of these meanings is primary the reference to Christ may be connoted. But the primary meaning of the verb *pisteuin* ["to have faith"] in specifically Christian usage is "the acceptance of the kerygma of Christ." [10]

Nor yet need we confine ourselves to Protestant theology. The Roman theologian Hans Küng argues a *nihil obstat* of Catholic orthodoxy for this notion of faith. He is aware of the dangers. Perhaps, he says, it means a "faithful trust, not primarily an assent to abstract truths but an affirmation of a person." [11]

The only way in which these conceptions of faith can be reconciled with the evidence of the Synoptic Gospels is by insisting that the questions be pursued: What does this "faithful trust" (Küng) add up to? How does a man "accept the kerygma of Christ" (Bultmann)? The Gospels say "trust" is action; "accepting the kerygma" is action. It is not a settled state, but a momentary deed. It is not a door into a place that will be constantly occupied thereafter, but a blind leap into a river, quickly to come out again! It is not a saying, "Lord, I believe, help my unbelief," as if once it had happened, all would be well. Nor yet can we say it is a "moment by moment reliance on God," for that is no more possible or relevant for us than it would have been for Jesus or the disciples who had, as we saw at first, a whole lot of businesses of living to get on with, *within which* God was hidden, but also within which things other than "faith" were needed to see them through.

We now turn to discipleship.

(3) *Discipleship: The continuation of Jesus' work.*

[10] Rudolf Bultmann, *Theologisches Wörterbuch zum Neuen Testament* (Stuttgart, 1960), VI, 209.

[11] *Justification* (Camden, N. J.: Thomas Nelson & Sons, 1964), p. 255.

We may discern at least five characteristics of discipleship as presented to us in the Gospels.

(a) *Discipleship consists in "being with Jesus."* Mark 3: 14 gives the first part of its threefold description of discipleship as "he appointed twelve, to be with him," or "as his companions" (NEB). The whole Gospel story is the story of Jesus and these men, of the destiny which the Lord first acted out and which, through their adherence to him, became their destiny also. Discipleship is Jesus-related existence. That is the first thing to say. The disciple is not the important person: Jesus is—Jesus and his "work." The Jesus to whom the disciple is thus "discipled" is Christ not through "status" ("Are you the Christ?"), but through activity, through deeds. Therefore, to be a disciple is to be "with" Christ in his deeds. This is the significance of Caesarea Philippi—not that the disciples come to conclude something about Jesus' messiahship, but that that messiahship is revealed as a *way,* a destiny, a deed, which is to be completed and which is then to become the way, destiny, and deed of the disciple (Mark 8:27-38).

(b) *Discipleship is the healing ministry.* The disciple is to carry out the ministry of Jesus in meeting others' needs. This is in the Gospels primarily as the mission to "cast out demons" (Mark 3:15), that is, to heal. If we compare Mark 6:7-12; Luke 9:1-5, and Matthew 10:1, 8, 12, we find that the three factors mentioned as being the content of his own mission by Jesus in his message to John (Matt. 11:4-5) are found also in the disciples' mission. Thus, power, *exousia,* over unclean spirits (Matthew, Mark), power of healing (Matthew, Luke) and preaching (in all three, though not as an instruction in Mark) feature in the disciples' mission as they do in the Lord's. Their healing power, again, was not a pneumatic power of their own, but the use of the "name" of Jesus and possibly also the repetition of the words used by him in healing. The content of the disciples' message in the texts just cited is given as "that men should repent" (Mark —as for John the Baptist), "the kingdom of God" (Luke —as with Jesus, Luke 4:43), and saying that "the kingdom of heaven is at hand" (Matthew, cf. Matt. 4:23, for Jesus). The continuation of the work and message of Jesus in the persons of the twelve is in Luke 10:17 and Acts 2:43 ff. It is also implied by such sayings as Mark 13:34.[12]

(c) Discipleship is not simply a matter of this or that person "choosing" to be a disciple. *Discipleship is a "way,"* which many do not tread who claim to be followers or applauders. "Why do you call me 'Lord, Lord,' and not do what I tell you?" (Luke 6:46.) Many will claim allegiance to him and will be denied by him (Matt. 7:21-23) because they have not performed his deeds. At the same time, there will be some who have never claimed allegiance to him who will find themselves accepted by him because their deeds coincided with his deeds. This is the implication of the parable of the judgment (Matt. 25:31-46). The thing to say about my neighbor is, "Well, I must be careful, for he might be serving Christ if he does Christ's deeds" (Luke 9:49). The thing to say about myself is, "My volitional commitment to Christ does not mean that I am his disciple and that he will own me" (Luke 11:23). Discipleship consists in fulfilling Christ's way and is acknowledged only and always when it does so. I never know when another's attitude *to me* makes him a disciple (Matt. 25:40).

The disciple's task is to describe and indicate the way, to point to the meaning of all in Christ. The disciple himself becomes crucial for the whole christological economy by participating in Christ's lordship and by pointing towards it.

(d) *Discipleship implies suffering and deprivation at the*

---

[12] Cf. John Coutts, "The Authority of Jesus and the Twelve," *Journal of Theological Studies* (NS), VIII (1957), 111-18.

hands of the world. The mission of the Master had necessitated this, and so does that of the disciple. This disciple is to "take up his cross" (Mark 8:34), which seems to mean a conscious and willing parting with everything which ministers to his own egocentricity, such as family, livelihood, possessions, and status (Luke 14:26-27; Matt. 10:37). It also means the willing acceptance of part in the messianic sufferings of the Master at the hands of the world. This is the "cup" of Christ, which the disciples suggest they might drink (Mark 10:38 ff.), the "fire" with which they are to be salted (Mark 9:49), the "baptism" with which they are to be baptized (Mark 10:38). The contexts of the sayings about the disciples being "salt" likewise make it plain that the essential element, the salt, which is necessary, is complete discipleship with its consequent self-renunciation; and in these sayings also the aim of the "saltiness" becomes plain— notably, the usefulness of the disciples and of discipleship to the world (Mark 9:47-50; Luke 14:26-35; Matt. 5:11-13).[18]

It should be noted that the suffering of the disciple in meeting the discipleship demands upon himself and also the suffering which the world metes out to the disciple as he goes about his Master's will are both, as it were, prerequisites and consequences of discipleship, though they are not themselves discipleship. Discipleship is the continuing of the deeds and ministry of Jesus. The cross comes as the means to and the result of this discipleship. The Christian vocation to suffering, to "complete what is lacking in Christ's afflictions" (Col. 1:24), is only part of the wider ministry of redemption, healing, and reconciliation to which the disciple is called.

(e) *Discipleship is participation in Christ's hidden lordship.* The picture of the twelve sitting on thrones, judging (Matt.

[18] Oscar Cullmann, "Que signifie le sel dans la parabole de Jésus?" *Revue d'histoire et de philosophie religieuses,* XXXVII (1957), 36-43.

19:28), whatever its original form, implies that the disciple stands in a decisive position between Christ the Lord and the world over which he is Lord. In fact, the parables of stewardship (Luke 12:13-21, 17:7-10, 19:11-27) may be taken to imply that the disciple's prime concern is not with his own self-preservation or purity but with the right management of God's affairs in his world. The disciple stands in a position of dual responsibility in the world. Before God, he stands representing man, which means intercession. Before man, he stands representing God, which means witness. Thus, it is his task to try to insure that, somehow or other, God gets done in his world what he requires to be done.

This the disciple does, not by "political action," which was excluded for him because of the political situation in which the Christians stood, but by repeating his Master's words. Hence, the disciples' words are of great importance. The disciple, indeed, is the one who hears the word of God and holds on to it (Luke 11:28), that is, remembers and lives by it. Sayings like these incline one to think that Jesus taught his disciples to learn his message *by heart*.[14] This was not simply for the disciple's own sake, but also because he must pass on the "words." Every idle or unnecessary word will be judged (Matt. 12:36-37). The disciple is the one who understands the meaning of the words which are spoken to him by the Master (Matt. 19:11, Mark 4:11-20) He is to "ponder my words" (Luke 9:44 NEB), that is, remember them and try to discern their meaning when remembered and thought over. Thus, after the resurrection, the disciples are reminded of the things he had said (Luke 24:44-49). "Teaching them to observe all that I have commanded

[14] Cf. my paper, "Did Jesus Teach His Disciples to Learn by Heart?" pp. 105-18, from which three paragraphs are included above. Cf. in general, Birger Gerhardsson, *Memory and Manuscript: Oral Tradition and Written Transmission in Rabbinic Judaism and Early Christianity* (Lund, 1961).

you" is Matthew's summary of the disciples' message (Matt. 28:20).

The purpose of this repeating the Master's message on the part of the disciple is clear. The disciples' words are regarded as having the same significance for judgment as those of the Master. "He who hears you hears me" (Luke 10:16) can surely mean nothing else than that the disciples were to memorize and repeat the message their Master taught. Rejection or acceptance of the disciple meant rejection or acceptance of the disciple's Lord. (Matt. 10:40 has "receive" for "hear" in the parallel verse to Luke 10:16.) Christ is making his appeal through the disciples (II Cor 5:20). His lordship is being exercised on earth, partly at least, through their words. Thus, in Luke 21:15, the disciples are promised: "I will give you a mouth and wisdom, which none of your adversaries will be able to withstand or contradict." Faithful hearing and memorizing will be rewarded by the ability to utter what is remembered and the insight to understand it when the time comes. In the meantime, the words must be heard and held on to.

And this, it seems, is exactly what happened. The disciples did "learn" the sayings or parables, but did not understand them. From the point of view of Jesus, they are admitted into the "secrets" of the kingdom (Mark. 4:11; Luke 8:10; Matt. 13:11). And the fact that they are admitted at all implies that they will be given more and more of those secrets (Mark 4:25; Luke 8:18; Matt. 13:12). However, the disciples do not understand. They do not see any further than the incomprehending crowds (Mark 4:12-13, 7:18) and are described as they are (Mark 8:18)—part of a faithless generation (Mark 9:19). Mark follows each announcement of the passion with a debate of complaint and incomprehension from the disciples (Mark 8:31–9:1, 9:31-50, 10:33-45). They have to be warned against the "leaven of the Pharisees and the leaven of Herod" (Mark 8:15); they harden their hearts (Mark 6:52, 8:17), just as the Jewish authorities (Mark 3:5, 10:5). These comments are, of course, toned down by Luke and Matthew. But what must lie behind them? The answer lies surely, in the fact that the disciples were taught mysteries which they had to "hear" and "become part of" (enter into), sayings which they must "hold on to," which they were obliged to repeat in the lifetime of Jesus even though they did not understand them. These mysteries and sayings are then "recalled" in the early church, with the Holy Spirit (if we may so put it) enlightening them as to the contemporary implications of the sayings—such, at any rate, seems to be Luke's theory (Luke 12:12).

John, as usual, systematizes it all and loses some of the mystery and the magic. The Paraclete will come after Jesus has left them, to "teach you all things, and bring to your remembrance all that I have said to you" (John 14:26), to "guide you into all the truth;" . . . [and] "take what is mine, and declare it to you" (John 16:13-14). The disciples' misunderstanding will all be cleared (John 12:16). One cannot help feeling that something has been lost when the identification of disciple and Lord is stressed in mystical terms (John 14–15). John is right that the resurrection is the time for the clear "participation in Christ's lordship," but the *mode* of that participation is precisely the issue on which, by systematizing the hints of the Synoptics, he in fact loses much that they are saying. All the Gospels, in Bengel's phrase, "breathe the resurrection." To participate in Christ's lordship in the midst of the way of discipleship is already to know the imprimatur of resurrection resting on the manifestations of love in the midst of the world.

Chapter 11

RESURRECTION: JESUS OUR CONTEMPORARY

The earliest Christian message was "Jesus." It was not a separable proclamation about Jesus. It was that all that Jesus began both to do and to teach from the beginning (Acts 1:1) was now released into life again. The best statement of this, and the one least overloaded with later dogmatization, is in Acts 2:22-24 (NEB):

I speak of Jesus of Nazareth, a man singled out by God and made known to you through miracles, portents, and signs, which God worked among you through him, as you well know. When he had been given up to you, by the deliberate will and plan of God, you used heathen men to crucify and kill him. But God raised him to life again, setting him free from the pangs of death, because it could not be that death should keep him in its grip.

Jesus is first of all the "man singled out by God"; he is the anointed, selected, approved one. Jesus is the one made known through miracles and signs. Jesus is crucified "by God's deliberate plan," but no soteriological purpose for this is stated. The reason why he has been brought back to life is plain. The resurrection, not the cross, is the center of the whole proclamation, and the reason for the resurrection was that it simply could not be that death could keep him in its grip, a man who was what he was. The whole of the rest of Acts is about Jesus who has "poured out this" (Acts 2:33), who now reenacts, in the person of his followers, the same activities as in the days in Galilee.[1]

The word "gospel" (*evangelion*) is the word "good news," which Jesus is said to have preached (*kerysso*) at the beginning of Mark's Gospel: "After John was arrested, Jesus came into Galilee, preaching the gospel of God, and saying, 'The time is fulfilled, the kingdom of God is at hand; repent, and believe in the gospel'" (Mark 1:14-15). Thus the preaching (*kerygma*) of Jesus was the good news (*evangelion*) that the kingdom had come (*eggizo*—to come near, to arrive at a place, rather than to go into it!—we pass by an almost incessant scholarly dispute in a word!). The word "kerygma" simply means "preaching." However, the word has also come to be used by both C. H. Dodd in England and Bultmann and others in Germany to indicate also the *content* of the preaching of the early church, a proclamation of the acts of God in Jesus Christ.[2] Unfortunately, the kerygmatic summaries of Acts were never meant to be taken as complete statements of Christian faith. Many of them say nothing at all about the Jesus who is the subject of the kerygma. This was understandable in Palestine, as everyone knew at least

---

[1] Cf. in general, on this and what follows, E. J. Tinsley, *The Imitation of God in Christ* (London: SCM Press, 1960), pp. 106-17; and Walter Künneth, *Theology of the Resurrection* (St. Louis: Concordia Press, 1965), pp. 130-32.

[2] *The Apostolic Preaching and Its Development* (New York: Harper & Row). On more recent developments, cf. Paul Althaus, *The So-called Kerygma and the Historical Jesus* (Edinburgh: Oliver and Boyd, 1959), pp. 19-37; J. M. Robinson, "Kerygma und Geschichte in Neuen Testament," *Zeitschrift für Theologie und Kirche*, LXII (1963), 294-337.

some of the stories of Jesus' deeds and ministry, so that the "kerygma about Jesus" was understandable because people knew what content to give to the word "Jesus." It is no longer the case today and was not the case as soon as the gospel preaching of the early church moved away from Jerusalem. The whole burden of the early church's preaching was not a summary statement of cross, resurrection, reign, and future coming, as if these were alone the "acts of God." It was first and foremost a proclamation of "the whole Jesus" who had been newly accredited by these later events. We shall say something in the next chapter about the *effect* of this overemphasis on a detachable kerygma. Here, we may simply say that the early church's good news (*evangelion*) which they preached (*kerysso*) was "Jesus," and not merely a summary statement of his post-Galilean history. Indeed, we may seriously question whether or not the early church, despite the summary statements in Acts (always suspect from a critical point of view), did not, like Jesus, preach (kerygma) in the form of teaching (*didache*).[3] It is probably far better not to use the word "kerygma" at all. It is not frequently used, even in Acts. The words "message" or "good news" indicate the total content of the early church's preaching and living far better; or, indeed, we could speak simply of the "earliest Christian *confessions*." [4]

Since the figure of Jesus was known in and around Jerusalem, naturally the center of the earliest gospel of the Christian church was the resurrection. "If Christ has not been raised, your faith is futile," cried Paul (I Cor. 15:17). The apostles were able to found the church because they could

---

[3] Cf. my paper, "Didactic Kerygma in the Synoptic Gospels," *Scottish Journal of Theology*, X (1957), 262-73.

[4] Cf. Oscar Cullmann, *The Earliest Christian Confessions;* and Werner Kramer, *Christ, Lord, Son of God* (Naperville, Ill.: Alec R. Allenson, 1966), pp. 45-55.

preach the resurrection of Jesus. This would have been impossible if the Jews had been able to point to the body. The accusation which in fact was made was that the disciples had stolen the body (Matt. 28:11-15; Justin Martyr, *Dialogue with Trypho*, 108). Had they done this, they would have been insincere in preaching the resurrection; and they would hardly have carried their deception to the point of dying for it, the more so since they did not stand by their Master in the days of his flesh.

The only way to deny these "events" is either to question the honesty of the witnesses or else to describe them as "an overly pronounced deviation," which makes it an event to which it is impossible to apply historical methods.[5] It seems impossible to do this in the light of the subsequent history of the church. Whatever, the "fact" was, there were undeniable and irrefutable *implications* in the lives of the disciples which are inexplicable apart from some "fact" which they called appearances of Jesus.

What, then, happened? "A series of subjective visions" based on the disciples' intimacy with Jesus prior to his crucifixion and on their faith that he proclaimed the word of God?[6] This would be completely out of accord with the whole story of the disciples as contained in the Gospels. Far more likely, they expected a resurrection of Jesus as the general resurrection when all the righteous would "shine like the brightness of the firmament; and . . . like the stars for ever and ever" (Dan. 12:3). Nothing predisposed them to expect a resurrection of Jesus prior to this general resurrection, any more than Martha expected one for Lazarus prior to the "resurrection at the last day" (John 11:24). Josephus says that most of the Jews adhered to the pharisaic teaching

[5] Marc Bloch, *The Historian's Craft* (New York: Alfred A. Knopf, 1953), p. 115.

[6] Bultmann, *Kerygma and Myth*, ed. H. W. Bartsch (New York: Harper & Row, 1961), I, 42.

of a resurrection (Josephus, *Antiquities,* 13.10.5; 18.1.3-4). Indeed, elements of this "general resurrection" have crept into the stories of Jesus' resurrection (Matt. 27:52). For all its problems, the resurrection cannot be dismissed. It has become, indeed, the linchpin for a new theology of historical-revelational positivism.[7]

If we persist with our search for the meaning of the Christian message, we would have to say that the resurrection seems to be the one place at which the whole thing becomes clear, falls into place. The resurrection, in itself, does not· add anything new. It merely (and importantly!) states that all that Jesus had been he now is forever; that the things which he said in the days of his flesh now belong to the eternal "word"; that the one whose life represented the hidden presence of the kingdom is now always doing the things he had done in his ministry.

That is, the resurrection points us back to the secular Jesus of the Gospels and cries, "This is now the Christ." The Jesus who was in the secular world is now the church's contemporary in the heavens!

This insistence upon the resurrection cannot be given any kind of scientific "apologia." The Western rational mind and the English pragmatic mind assail the evidence now with all the weapons of psychical research, depth psychology, and even the theory of relativity. But the resurrection events are, fortunately or unfortunately, not capable of proof or disproof in such terms. Indeed, we are left with a recognition of the impossibility of dealing with the resurrection phenomena in the New Testament in other than "dynamistic" categories. The New Testament itself invites such categories by insisting that the resurrection body had both physical and

[7] Wolfhart Pannenberg, *Grundzüge der Christologie* (Gütersloh: Gerhard Mohn, 1964), pp. 85-103; cf. D. P. Fuller, "The Resurrection of Jesus and the Historical Method," *Journal of Bible and Religion,* XXXIV (1966), 18-24.

nonphysical qualities—a situation utterly irresolvable along "scientific" lines, but entirely to be expected in view of the Gospels' consistent insistence that hiddenness and manifestation go hand in hand, and that only "the moment" can make plain (more or less!) what the *exousia* of God in Jesus will do, what the *dynamis* of the kingdom will demand.

Dr. George MacLeod brought from America the delightful story that some archaeologists had found the body of Jesus in a tomb in Palestine, "and just before Easter, too." Pope John XXIII hastily consulted the church leaders, then the theologians Bultmann, Barth, and Niebuhr. None of them knew what to do. Finally, Tillich was asked. His only reply on long-distance line to the Pope was: "Ze body! He really *lived*, then, did he?"

Well, whether or not, with Gregor Smith, "we may freely say that the bones of Jesus lie somewhere in Palestine," [8] there remains an insoluble problem. J. A. T. Robinson has recently reminded us that we are remarkably dishonest in our thinking about the resurrection body. He imagines himself asking J. B. Phillips or C. S. Lewis, with reference to the ascension:

"Do you really think the body went on through space, passing out of the gravitational pull, first of the earth, then of the sun, and that now, after two thousand light-years, it is somewhere in the middle of the Milky Way?" . . . Indeed, I suspect that many of us, if we are honest, try to have it both ways, and suppose that Jesus did literally go up in front of the disciples' eyes, but that directly he got out of sight it somehow ceased to be a physical event at all, and the thing was called off. [9]

Indeed, there is no solution this way. It is sufficient to say that the resurrection and ascension (for the two need to be

[8] *Secular Christianity* (New York: Harper & Row, 1966), p. 103.
[9] "Ascendancy," *New Christian*, May 19, 1966.

considered almost as a single event) mark the point at which, as we have said, the Jesus-event becomes, at least to the mind of faith, the Christ-event of all creation. This is not a "demonstration," nor after all the *deus ex machina;* for it is only given to the apostles and requires some perseverance before even they will believe. It does not fundamentally alter what we have said about faith and discipleship. Rather, it reasserts it. The healing had been available only to "faith" —as every man was confronted in his secularity by the hidden demand of the kingdom, the would-be disciple was expected to see in Jesus what no one else could see, and give up all in the hope of it. The three elements of faith, of action, and of discipleship, which we found in ch. 10 were to be seen in the Gospel confrontations with Jesus, and all these are now to be found in the confrontations with the risen Lord.

There is no conflict between the post-Easter "Christ of faith" and the precrucifixion "Jesus of history." The whole basis of Christianity is the early disciples' experience that the Jesus whom they understood by the resurrection appearances to have been made Lord and Christ was the same Jesus who had lived and taught among them from the beginning. Hence, they began to identify themselves also with those who had been with him in the flesh, and the habit spread to all who joined the church. Bornkamm speaks of the "anachronism" of the early church believing in and trusting its ascended Lord and at the same time feeling itself to be identified with those who walked and talked with Jesus in the days of his flesh. Faith could not be other than discipleship to the earthly Master in which cross and resurrection first confronted them. We may cite Fuchs to a similar effect, though criticizing Bornkamm:

Faith is Discipleship. And the faith-character of this discipleship of faith first becomes known and reliable in view of the cross of Jesus. On this view, the Easter faith is not the renewing of a "broken off" faith, as Bornkamm thinks, but the purifying and new confirmation of the faith which had already been present in discipleship.[10]

It is what we have called the "faith which works." Discipleship is inseparable from commitment and obedience—and that means action.

The early Christian message, then, was not mainly about the *cross.* We have sufficiently demonstrated that the Gospels are not merely "passion narratives with introductions," as Martin Kähler thought. We have seen throughout that the ministry and teaching of Christ must be given the proper and vital determinative place. Moreover, even if one followed Kähler, one would still have to ask, "Why all the story of the death of *this man,* more than any other? What in *him* made his passion so important to mankind?" To answer simply, "Because this was the one whom God raised from the dead," is merely to point further the question: Why this one?

Indeed, it is the growing conclusion of New Testament scholars that, whatever the particular statements of particular texts in the New Testament, the cross of Jesus is to be seen as secondary to his whole life, rather than his whole life as secondary to the cross. "Jesus crucified for me" has become the hallmark of piety, Western or Eastern, Protestant or Catholic. But its presence as a total view of Jesus in the New Testament is questionable; and certainly so far as the Gospels and Acts are concerned, the isolated text about the ransom (Mark 10:45) must be seen within the context of the atoning value of the death of the righteous—an idea far from absent in Paul—rather than in more conventional terms.[11] As for

[10] Ernst Fuchs, *Die Frage nach dem historischen Jesus* (Hamburg, 1959), p. 188 (not in *Studies of the Historical Jesus*).

[11] Cf. C. K. Barrett, "The Background of Mark 10.45," *New Testament Essays (in memory of T. W. Manson)* (Manchester: Manchester University Press, 1959), pp. 1-18.

the language of Paul, a recent essay has questioned whether the cross was in any sense the "place of atonement" in Paul's view. Much rather, the author claims, must we consider that God has made the historical man Jesus to be the place of his righteousness, the Jesus who in death and resurrection still holds grace for mankind in the new possibility of human existence.[12]

Or, it might be thought, have we not completely disregarded the question of the *eschatological* viewpoint of various Christian elements in the earliest church and the eschatological viewpoint of Jesus? It seems likely to me that Jesus expected the end of the world to be associated with his own vindication and that this in a physical sense did not happen. It also seems likely that the Gospels as we have them imply that Jesus may not have identified this "vindication" with his crucifixion/resurrection, but may have anticipated a time "between" that event and the Parousia—as W. G. Kümmel argues.[13] This expectation of a final vindication the earliest church continued in its anticipation of Christ coming on the clouds. However, by the time the Gospels were written, most Christians had begun to think of the present as the decisive time. Now, the problem for us is to know how far the eschatological sayings in the Gospels— which were written between A.D. 60 and 100—go back to the expectation of the church for which the Gospel in question was written, or to the view of the writer, or to the view of the piece of tradition he is handling at the time, or to the oral tradition between, say, A.D. 33 and 50—that is, the influence behind the piece of tradition as he had it, or to the memorization of the disciples, or, finally, to the Lord himself. When one has reached the latter, one then has to

[12] Gottfried Fitzer, "Der Ort der Versöhnung nach Paulus," *Theologische Zeitschrift*, XXII (1966), 161-84.

[13] *Promise and Fulfillment* (Naperville, Ill.: Alex R. Allenson, 1957).

ask whether Jesus himself meant what he said directly or indirectly; whether it was a straightforward statement or a parabolic one; and whether or not Jesus was mistaken or misunderstood from the very beginning. In any case, we probably overemphasize the depth of the early Christians' disappointment. Like the *Oracula Sibyllina* or the Qumran sectaries,

The apocalyptic circles of the New Testament had long been accustomed to such disappointments. When the Last Things did not occur at the expected time, they postponed the final date without excessive crises of re-orientation and anxiety.[14]

Interestingly, no part of the New Testament contains a trace of tradition that a specific date was ever given for the Parousia. Probably the story is too complicated to be unraveled now, despite all the scholarly efforts (mutually contradictory, unfortunately) at solving it.

My point at the moment is simply that we cannot assume that we know what the writers intended. Basically, they were ministering the traditions about Jesus, which they had received, to people who, in vastly differing situations and needs, looked to those traditions as the source of all things. The theologian at any time can do no other and no more— and dare do no less. Jesus is not to be tied inextricably to any one "context," as we have seen. Paul disappeared for three years before his version of the Jesus-drama became clear —and then he spoke it in fear and trembling, so different was it from what the apostles before him had taught (Gal. 1: 15–2:21). He was not the only one in New Testament times to see what he could see in Jesus and cry, "Hier stehe ich; ich kann nicht anders." It has been the recurring error of much of the so-called "New Testament theology" to imagine that

[14] Ethelbert Stauffer, *Jesus and His Story*, p. 183.

it could reconcile everything under this or that overall attitude. It cannot be done and ought not to be tried. All we can attempt in this book is to try one "line," and to show how certain things come alive through it. The "line" is what we have called "the whole Christ," the *totus Christus* of Martin Luther, the "Christ in all his offices" of John Wesley. All we do is to show what light comes from this fount. Basically, no New Testament writer did any different, although the *way* in which he did it might appear vastly strange by contrast.

The mention of Paul may bring another question to mind: Does Paul in fact appear as witness for the Jesus-centric resurrection message which we have described? The distinctive contribution of Paul to the discovery of the true significance of the Christ-events must not be minimized. But it is generally felt that the importance of the figure of Jesus to the apostle has often been underplayed by overemphasizing some of his *ways* of stating his Jesus-centricity (e.g. in the cross, as already mentioned). Nearly sixty years ago, Johannes Weiss wrote a book on the subject in which he showed that Paul's commands to unselfishness, renunciation, and so forth, are invariably made by appealing to the example of Christ (I Cor. 4:16-17; 10:24, 33; 11:1; Rom. 15:3; Phil. 2:5 ff.); that Paul's ethical system derives from his knowledge of the teaching of Jesus and only in small matters from Hellenistic thought; and that Paul's "confidence in his salvation" was directly related to "the religion of Jesus" and was not a "theoretical acceptance of the facts of salvation."[15] A recent writer, Eberhard Jüngel,[16] asks how far Jesus himself comes to speak anew in the "speech event" (*Sprachereignis*) of "Pauline teaching on justification." The Pauline

15 Johannes Weiss, *Paul and Jesus* (New York: Harper & Row, 1909), pp. 117-29.

16 *Paulus und Jesus*, pp. 3, 41.

teaching, he thinks, like the parables of Jesus, is a speech event of God's coming reign. This means that Paul is interested not only in the "fact" of Jesus, but also in the "facts" about Jesus.[17]

What the New Testament writers are saying, then, in their various and diverse ways is that they hold that the Jesus-events are now clearly (almost!) through the resurrection made into Christ-events; that the Jesus who "once came" now "lives and reigns"; that the Jesus of the Gospels is Jesus our contemporary.

Thus, the New Testament writers take with complete seriousness "all that Jesus began both to do and to teach." Admittedly, they spend much energy and space in proving the relationship of this to the Law, or to the sacrifices of the Temple, or to the Jewish practices of the day. But this is only because Jesus is the contemporary who now lives and reigns—both in the "now" of A.D. 68 and the "now" of 1968.

And if it is that secular Jesus of whom we read in the Gospels who now "lives and reigns," then the way in which he appears in the Gospel narratives is decisive for the way in which he now lives and reigns. He does not "live" in a way different from or contrary to his secular life in Palestine. He does not "reign" in a way different from his tentative and hidden and yet at times "dynamic" authority manifest in healing, judging, and calling men. His ministry is transformed, but it is not fundamentally altered. His mode of operation is enlarged, but it is not changed. What he began to do and teach he is now able to do and teach in fuller,

---

[17] The *Was*, not only the *Dass*. Cf. W. G. Kümmel, *New Testament Studies*, X (1964), 163-81, against W. W. Schmithals, *Zeitschrift für die neutestamentliche Wissenschaft*, LIII (1962), 145-60; both contain references to the current Jesus-Paul discussion. Cf. also J. P. Brown, *New Testament Studies*, X (1963), 27-48.

freer guise—not more openly, perhaps even less openly, but essentially the same.

Thus the authentic task for New Testament theology is to carry on the work which in fact the New Testament began but scarcely fulfilled—the work of taking the incarnation, healing, hiddenness, crucifixion, and resurrection of Jesus, and asking how Jesus the contemporary now operates these life-giving and mysterious ministries in the midst of the secular. This is a work which the New Testament never fulfilled, because so much of the writing of apostles and even evangelists (the form critics are surely right in insisting) had to be spent in looking backward into the Old Testament to show how Jesus ought to have been expected (we have seen flaws in their argument here); or outward into the world to show how Jesus separated his people from the world, the flesh, and the devil, particularly in the crudities of life in the Roman Empire (we may say that these moralizings have little to say to us as we do not live in the Roman Empire); or else inward within the church to try to keep the wayward at the game of Christian living (we shall not say here how deeply we sympathize with their problems!); or else, finally, onward to an "end" with God which becomes less and less clear as time goes on (the eschatologians will be always with us!).

But, behind all this, and often visible beneath it, the New Testament directs us to the one whom faith proclaims is Lord and Christ, and the points at which we today need to be faithful to the New Testament are the points of "christocentricity," not the points of "application." We do not live among people for whom Old Testament or Roman-morals or even church immorality, much less eschatology, are live issues. But we do live in the world. We live, too, in a world of need. We live among other people who must live. We live among people who suffer. We live in the hope of meaningfulness. The New Testament proclaims that world means incarnation, that need means healing, that life means hiddenness, that suffering means identification, that meaningfulness means resurrection. Christianity is the claim that this kind of pattern of existence, summarized in incarnation, healing, hiddenness, crucifixion, and resurrection, holds the whole universe, the whole cosmos together. The New Testament, indeed, begins to say it.

(1) *All things are made by Christ* (John 1:3). By him, all things are created (Col. 1:16). Whatever has life has him! All that man has, all nature, all science, is good. The earth is the Lord's and the fullness thereof (Ps. 24:1). The earth is not simply a background against which God and man play their games. The earth is itself the Lord's and in Christ God has reconciled the whole universe to himself (Col. 1:20). In Christ, man is shown how the earth can be restored to the one who has made it. In Christ, all the "secrets" of the world, "all [God's] treasures of wisdom and knowledge" (Col. 2:2-3) lie hidden.

(2) *All men are found in him.* All men will be brought to life in him (I Cor. 15:22). In him is life, and this life is the light of men (John 1:4). God has reconciled us men to himself through Christ (II Cor. 5:18); he has reconciled the whole cosmos (vs. 19). Jesus, the one true steward, comes to show man, whose stewardship defaulted in the garden of Eden, how he may yet be a steward of creation. There is no question now of differences between human beings of different races, religions, or classes, for Christ is now "all, and [is] in all" (Col. 3:11).

(3) *All things hold together in him* (Col. 1:17). In him, all things cohere. He upholds all things by his word of power (Heb. 1:3). All things have been put under Christ by God (I Cor. 15:28). The universe, all in heaven and on earth, has been brought to a unity in Christ (Eph. 1:10). Now,

they are all under the same head. Every power and authority in the universe is subject to him (Col. 2:10). Christ is the healer, engaged in bringing not ideal solutions to clear situations but rather a rescue operation, a holding operation, a healing operation. As Tertullian said of the church, so we may say of Christ, that he is the *glue* of society, that which holds the whole together.

(4) *All things find their end in him,* for there will be an "end" when all other powers will disappear before the kingdom and when Christ will deliver up the kingdom to the father (I Cor. 15:24). Christ has been appointed "heir of all things" (Heb. 1:2), and there will be a time when he will be all in all (Col. 3:11). All things will be made subject to him (I Cor. 15:28). God is a politician. He is engaged in drawing all humanity, all the world, all systems, all existence, all motivations and ideas and purposes into an end described as the kingdom of God. Then the desert shall blossom as the rose (Isa. 35:1), and the wolf shall lie down with the lamb (Isa. 11:6). At times, in faith, the Christian works backward from this future end.

(5) Finally, there is the promise for the "pale, unbelieving believer." *All things are yours:* all things—Paul, Apollos, Cephas (denominations already in the church of A.D. 45— how soon the inheritance got tainted!), the world, life, death, the present, the future—everything belongs to you (I Cor. 3:22-23)—the gift of significance, of eternal life. And thus, the Christian is taught to see in himself the "first fruits" (James 1:18; Rom. 8:23) of God's reconciling work (Col. 1:21-23). From now on, he works from Christ outward. He seeks to recognize that, hidden within the situations which confront him, there is always the possibility of ultimate significance, the kingdom of God. And this judges all preliminary efforts on his part to do the right thing or to use the right motivation, to bring healing and wholeness to life. All

this he does because of what he himself has received, comforting others with the comfort he has himself received from Christ (II Cor. 1:4). For as a mere man, he is dead; his life is hid with Christ in God (Col. 3:3).

This theology of the cosmic ministries of Christ is the point at which a good deal of writing has taken place.[18] Unfortunately, it is also the point at which the theologian easily becomes heady and imprecise. In particular, two matters must be stressed. In the first place, the temptation must be resisted to make the whole thing too systematic. In many of the texts we have named, it is quite impossible to draw any uniform or consistent picture out of the New Testament insights because they are insights—and insights of faith—and because they each use widely different thought worlds. The early Christian theology was not *centered* on anything other than the *continuing ministry* of the exalted Jesus of Nazareth.[19]

In the second place, the "cosmic" must be seen in the light of the Gospels. The fivefold "all things" of the developing New Testament in fact only seeks to put in *cosmic* terms—and does this sufficiently—the things that the Gospels put in *secular* terms. As we have observed throughout, the Gospels are theological documents. They were written by men who believed, and for communities which believed, that what happened in the secular story of Jesus of Nazareth was now happening through Jesus the risen and ascended Lord, who was now their contemporary. All too often, the form critics have wanted to make this point in a negative way—that

[18] Cf. Alan D. Galloway, *The Cosmic Christ* (London: SCM Press, 1955); Otto A. Pilschneider, *Christus Pantokrator: Vom Kolosserbrief zur Ökumene* (Berlin: Käthe Vogt, 1962); and Wilhelm Michaelis, *Die Versöhnung des Alls* (Bern, 1950).

[19] Thus resurrection of *Jesus*, hope in *Jesus*, are central. This seems to need stressing at times against Wolfhart Pannenberg and Jürgen Moltmann, *Theologie der Hoffnung* (Munich: Chr. Kaiser Verlag, 1964).

because the Gospels were written by those who worshiped the "Christ of faith" rather than the Jesus of history (we have insisted on the New Testament's identity between the two), the incidents and records, therefore, are historically questionable. I wish to make the point in a positive way. Because the incidents had been so securely seen and experienced in the secular, historical situation of the earthly Jesus, and because the church now proclaims that this same Jesus now sits at the right hand of God, then all that he began to do on earth, he now does again.

Chapter 12

SALVATION: THE GIFT OF SIGNIFICANCE

We have completed our study, fragmentary and incomplete though it is, of some of the evidence of the Gospel writers. What does it all add up to? What is it all about?

Answers abound. Many of them derive so directly from New Testament words and thought forms as to deceive us almost into believing that to repeat what the New Testament says is to be loyal to what the New Testament wants to say.

The debate about demythologizing is obviously the most significant attempt in this century to answer the question: What is it all about? We shall come to our own answer by means of a discussion of this debate.

For a start, we may say that we stand neither for nor against Bultmann's position. As a matter of fact, the contemporary theological scene is still far too much dominated by whether or not someone "follows" Bultmann. John Macquarrie is accused by Schubert Ogden of using the phrase "not only . . . but also" too much (long before the B.B.C.

canonized it!) [1] Macquarrie has little difficulty in showing that this is a far healthier refrain than Ogden's "completely," which he used five times in six pages! [2] The method of the present book is both more diletanttish and more systematic/ dogmatic, more all-embracing and more exclusive! It seeks at times to "drag out" statements which were not initially written with the intention of being dragged out in our direction. It also seeks to say things "completely"! The method will reveal itself, if it has not already been noticed, in the discussion which follows.

There is, of course, a certain obvious sense in which de-mythologization is absolutely unavoidable. Faced with the question, "Is Christianity any longer justified in speaking mythologically in a secularized world where mythological thinking is no longer necessary?" the obvious reply is "no." There is no point in going on saying things which are non-sense to the person addressed.

But this perhaps obscures the real problems. Mythological speech is the only one available if one is trying to say that the meaning of an event is not immediately obvious from a simple or analytical view. In Bultmann's words, a "myth" is simply a story which makes objective what is beyond objective experience, which uses "imagery to express the other worldly in terms of this world and the divine in terms of human life, the other side in terms of this side." [3] To a certain extent therefore, all speech which is other than purely descriptive of obvious or provable facts, and thus is "scientific," must be "mythological." It all depends upon what is meant by "other worldly" and "divine."

The kind of myth discovered is inevitably determined by

[1] Ogden, *Christ Without Myth* (New York: Harper & Row, 1961), p. 137.

[2] Macquarrie, *Studies in Christian Existentialism*, p. 157.

[3] Bultmann, *Kerygma and Myth*, I, 10. John Knox, *Myth and Truth* (Charlottesville: The University of Virginia Press, 1964), defines myth as "an account of an action of God," "a narrative cosmically significant but tied to human life."

preconceptions derived either from the world which produced the myth or from some other world. Bultmann says that the New Testament myth was determined by an apocalyptic world view which is untenable today. John Robinson says we need to lose the myths of God "up there" and "out there."

However, the myth does not necessarily "go against" the secular, but rather uses the secular as illustration and hence *extends* it. Indeed, it may be said, in some sense, that the "secularized world" finds it necessary to use myth. The "other worldly" is the area precisely in which mechanical processes take over—in which the computer reigns. The "other worldly" is the area in which atomic physics lands us by its reduction of all that is visible and tangible to the level of the invisible and intangible. Myth is the language used, then, to explain the unknown or the not directly known in terms of the more directly known.

Bultmann's great work was to attempt to remove the New Testament myth—the old "bottle"—so that the essential element—the new wine—could be seen for what it was. The mythical terms used in the New Testament obscure the real purpose behind them. We need new terms which will explain the "understanding of existence" which the myth was supposed to make plain; for the myth explains it no more. We must therefore discover what the myth is and take it away. The myth was above all *eschatological* and *apocalyptic*. The message of Jesus was that the eschatological issues could be presently reckoned with by entering into the salvation which will finally be revealed. This, the early church preached, had already happened in the death and resurrection of Jesus. In hearing this "kerygma" and appropriating it, people themselves became "saved." The first demythologizer was John, who said that the resurrection of Jesus, Pentecost, and the Parousia of Jesus are one and the same event, and those who believe already have "eternal life." Thus, to demythologize is to reject the world view of the New Testament and to put the essential meaning into a contemporary world view. This contemporary world view, to Bultmann, is the existentialist understanding of man and his life. What is left is the kerygma, the essential thing to be preached—that Jesus died, rose, and lives (whatever its existential meaning). Here Bultmann is with Dodd and the older biblical theologians in imagining a set verbal form of words (the kerygma) which has saving effect when heeded.

A while back, Fritz Buri wrote an article[4] in which he suggested that what we now needed to do was to take away the kerygma in order to get at the essential core. Why retain this relic of the myth? In fact, as Ernst Fuchs says, *all that the kerygma says is already in what Jesus said;* so that we now need the Gospels and the historical Jesus *first,* for the kerygma points to them. This is fine. But we now have to go even further. Do we need the kerygma to point? Does not the kerygma point to the least helpful and most mythical part of it all—the cross? From many points of view, the kerygma notion has probably served its time in theology. Even were it airtight as a theological notion, its effect has been simply to reinforce traditional Protestant verbalism, "orthodoxy," and antisocial actionism.[5]

[4] "Entmythologisierung oder Entkerygmatisierung der Theologie?" in *Kerygma und Mythos* (Hamburg, 1952) II, 85-101. Cf. his *Weg des Glaubens* (Munich, 1958) for his later position. Buri is debated by Ogden, *Christ Without Myth,* pp. 122-30.

[5] Cf. Amos W. Wilder, "A Kerygmatic Social Ethic," *Studies in the Background of the New Testament and Its Eschatology* (Cambridge: Cambridge University Press, 1960), pp. 509-36. Also, in general, Robert A. Bartels, *Kerygma or Gospel Tradition* (Minneapolis: Augsburg, 1961); and R. H. Fuller, *The New Testament in Current Study* (New York: Charles Scribner's Sons, 1962), pp. 54-60. This criticism remains true of what has been described as the "New Hermeneutic." The concentration of interest remains upon the words, the preaching, the kerygma. Cf. Ernst Fuchs, "The New Testament and the Hermeneutical Problem," in *The New Hermeneutic,* ed. J. M. Robinson and J. B. Cobb (New York: Harper & Row, 1964), pp. 111-45; and Eberhard Jüngel in *Theologische Literaturzeitung,* XCI (1960), 329-38. Also Gerhard

In fact, the kerygma is what the Germans call the "Word." Bultmann is first and last not a demythologizer but a Lutheran. "The message" must at all costs remain. Or else what is there to which people are to respond? But, of course, the message is the cross.

We need first to get clear what the "myth" is. The myth is not merely the bits in first century cosmology which we do not like, not merely the *deus ex machina* that Robinson dislikes, but the whole Christ story. To subtract anything is to subtract all. But to retain anything (as Bultmann does) is to raise the question: Why not retain all? Why only retain what suits your Lutheranism (the kerygma) and your existentialism (the assessment of the human situation)? Why not retain *all?* That is, what is it *all* about?

The kerygma must be demythologized. The setting of Jesus within first-century apocalypticism is only one part of this problem. We also need to lose the setting of Jesus within a framework of personal salvation expectation which in fact represents only a subsidiary part of the biblical story, but whose reduction into "personal faith" is exactly the place where Bultmann is merely a loyal preacher of Pauline "salvation by faith." As we have seen, Paul well knew the peculiarity within Christian thinking of "his Gospel." Well he knew the singularity of his own experience of "faith." Yet these have become the classic theology of Protestantism, the much boasted legacy of the first Reformation, the kerygma which must be retained at all costs.

Essentially, to "demythologize" is not to think that there is some element which can be extracted from the myth and which can be given separate existence as some kind of "truth." Rather is it to keep telling the story, the myth, keep acting out the symbol, and repeatedly to draw out their present

Ebeling, "Word of God and Hermeneutic," *ibid.,* pp. 78-110; and *Theology and Proclamation* (Philadelphia: Fortress Press, 1966).

implication, knowing that the latter hangs wholly upon the singularity of the former, but knowing too that to claim that "all things belong to Christ" is to demand that it really be "all things" and not the personal acceptance of the kerygma alone.

The claim of Christianity is that nothing can be known of the "other side" save what can be seen in the "this side," that is, in the man Jesus who stands before us. Bultmann writes:

Myth is an expression of man's conviction that the origin and purpose of the world in which he lives are to be sought, not within it, but beyond it—that is, beyond the realm of known and tangible reality—and that this realm is perpetually dominated and menaced by those mysterious powers which are its source and limit.[6]

Against this, Christianity asserts, point for point: Christology is the conviction that the origin and purpose of the world in which man lives are not to be sought beyond it but within it—that is, within the realm of known and tangible reality—and that this realm is perpetually dominated and menaced by that mysterious power which is its source and limit, notably Christ (for all other powers have been made subject to him). In other words the Christology is the myth. And the Christology is also the "truth" behind the myth. To be a Christian is to be lost in it, to see myself as visible, meaningful, accepted, and significant only in it and through it, crying, "Only look on us as found in him": in *him,* the *man,* who now "lives and reigns"; in him, the *truth* (acceptable life on earth) and the *myth* (the life, death, resurrection).

Thus we need to repeat the whole story, not just the kerygma: the Jesus—on the one hand the essence, the truth; on the other hand the myth, the symbol—in a form both "totally demythologized" and simultaneously "totally positiv-

6 Bultmann, *Kerygma and Myth,* I, 10-11.

ist" (if we may use opposed slogans to stake out the ground for the view we are trying to get).

What is it all about?

What God principally does in Jesus is to show mankind the way in which human life can be significant. He demonstrates in the person and deeds of Jesus the one response which he is able to accept. Demythologized, this means that he declares to every man the method whereby now every man may attain meaningfulness. The mythological statement of this is that this or that man is "saved" in the present and will be "saved" in the future. But this is only the mythological statement of it. The thing which is thus mythicized is that any man can now be accepted if he is "with Jesus," "in Christ"—that is, participating in the life of suffering, self-sacrifice, and service which is historically represented in the history of Jesus and to which God gave his once-for-all imprimatur in the resurrection.

What does it mean? If it is right, it means that every man already stands in the presence of God on earth. In human existence, every man, relationship, situation, nation, society, and class is confronted by practical and decisive issues demanding certain courses of action. Each issue is truly "existential," because it is a hidden manifestation of the issue with which Christ himself dealt and now deals. Each issue is thus an issue of life or death—the bringing of healing by willing participation in Christ, or else the death of the personality which refuses to have its existence and significance so determined. Christ is the way whereby the mundane, the secular, the human can be given the gift of ultimate significance. Various terms are used for this—"salvation," "the kingdom," "eternal life." To "believe" is to "trust" that this is really true by being prepared to be lost in actions which will only either "work" or "be justified" if, in fact, it is true. "Faith" in the New Testament is the preparedness to act as if the utterly unprovable—that God accepts what belongs to Christ—were true. It is to "act boldly," as if the hidden were already plain.

The myth, the symbol, is thus the effectual, prophetic sign of the gift of God which is both *discriminatory,* restricting itself to the deeds which are found to belong to Christ, and also *indiscriminate,* because all stand equally before the opportunity of acceptance and entry. The Christian's only "advantage" is that he *knows* what in fact applies to all. The atonement is the classic way of saying that the Christ deed now stands between all men and God. All men equally share in the benefits of his passion. All men now equally stand before the opportunity to become conscious disciples to it. This alone is what "being a Christian" or "joining the church" can mean in relation to this essential Christology.

Is it too far out? It is hardly further away from the New Testament than the evangelical notion that by a personal "leap of faith," I can avail myself of the salvation preached in the kerygma, which is the Protestant salvation myth still perpetuated by Bultmann and his followers.

Does it remove the "personal" element? Obviously, it removes the personal element in the sense of evangelical or catholic piety—in the sense of a settled personal relationship which is established by faith and maintained in some "spiritual realm." But this is not to "depersonalize the gospel." It is to insist that the personal shall find its place within the whole context of real life. The person works from inwardness outward in the realm of nature; from "saving my soul" to "bearing witness to it in the world outside." But in the realm of Christ, the movement is from the outside, the secular, where Christ is, to the inside, the personal, where the individual is. When Jesus says that there is no saving of man's life from the inside toward the outside, this is surely what he means. Only the man who has actually lost any sense of his own "life" because of Jesus will save it.

But, it might be thought, to call salvation "the gift of significance" makes it all too hard. Ordinary wayfaring people will not be able to make any sense out of it. Yet, as we have seen, Jesus accepted three groups of people. First, there were those who in order to share in the benefits of the kingdom were called to take up the cross and follow, which meant either open allegiance to him or a complete change in their life. The second group were those incapable of doing so, who received the mercy of God and were healed. The third group, those who apparently were accepted for any other reason, were in fact accepted because they had discerned and responded to the issue of the hidden kingdom—that is, discipleship, significance—without knowing it. Ernst Percy says, "Discipleship is the greatest of all possible offerings and is decisive for participation in salvation." [7] "Salvation," as we have seen, is not often on Jesus' lips. He only uses the word once—of Zacchaeus' giving away his possessions (Luke 19:9). Apart from that, "salvation" belongs to the Last Day. Zacchaeus has simply anticipated the issue of his judgment.

Extra scholam domini nulla salus. Participation in the cross, the deed of our redemption, is the only way. Jesus' deed "for me" must also become my deed "with him." "Nothing the disciple does *binds* God as Jesus' deed or that of his righteous forbears bound God." [8] But Jesus' "for me" alone can easily make me careless. My "with him" alone can make me self-sufficient. But without my deed I cannot be received by him. The disciple's cross is not a "supererogatory work," an optional extra. It is the only acceptable response to the Lord's cross.

It was probably inevitable that Christianity should become

[7] *Die Botschaft Jesu* (Lund, 1953), p. 174.

[8] Braun, *Radikalismus*, II, 43.

a religion of salvation. In the sense of Christ's efficacious life for all, it is such. Salvation in that sense has already been obtained for all. In the sense of future survival through judgment, again, we may speak of "salvation." That is a mystery hidden from us at present. But in the sense so dear to evangelical Christianity—that of a present enjoying of salvation in the assurance of the "Savior's" past, present, and future work "for us"—we can find nothing in the words of Jesus.[9] One can, indeed, and must enter personally into the mystery of salvation now by participating in the fellowship of Christ's sufferings. But that is all. The only answer to inquiries about eternal life is "follow me" (Mark 10:17, 21) —and leave the future to God. The disciple is discipled ultimately to a kingdom which he may himself never enjoy. Discipleship is not the same thing as salvation or entering the kingdom, in the sense that both of these belong to the future or to the hidden meaning of man's life.

Consequently, Jesus, assuming such a "realm of significance" open to every man, puts the complete emphasis upon man's response. As Ernst Percy has put it, while for Paul obedience is the *result* of receiving salvation, for Jesus "reception of his message and obedience to God's will are the same." Indeed, sometimes it is "love your enemies so that you may be sons of your Father" (Matt. 5:44-45).[10] It cannot be denied that the emphasis often is "Do this, and God will be faithful," rather than "be faithful for God has done this."

But, it will be objected, this theology in fact ends up by setting works above faith; it merely sets the way of Jesus against that of Paul. But there is no conflict between Paul and Jesus. However, this is not because Paul's fideism is in the Gospels, but because Paul's theology is not fideism. Man-

<hr />

[9] Cf. my *Christ and Methodism*, pp. 15-20.

[10] Percy, *Die Botschaft Jesu*, pp. 114-15.

son may be right to see a "direct (conscious?) contrast to such a passage as Rom. 10:9" ["If you confess with your lips that Jesus is Lord . . . you will be saved."] in Gospel sayings like Matt. 7:21 ["Not every one who says to me, 'Lord, Lord,' . . ."].[11] Doubtless, Luke 6:46: "Why do you call me, 'Lord, Lord,' . . ." is a more original form. But it should never be forgotten that the early church managed to live in the midst of this so-called "war." And in the personal lives of Christians, we may be sure that there was no difference between the Christian who relied on faith and the one who relied on works, because in fact what they both relied on was Christ. Their "relying" itself was neither faith nor work, but their relationship to Christ, that is, their *discipleship,* their "being saved by his life" (Rom. 5:10).

If the law/gospel dichotomy is insisted upon, then we must say that every man is "saved" not by his taking Christ as gospel, but by his taking him as law. To take him as law is constantly to be thrown back on him as gospel, for he is himself the only way to obey the new Torah. Moreover, Jesus is not the same as the old Torah even if only because no man can now sit down and try to work out how he can remain "blameless in the law." It has been one of the failures of Protestant theology to assume that Jesus either rejected law in favor of grace or else merely elaborated the OT Law and left us where we were before; except that happily, Christianity began with Paul. We hope that we have shown that both alternatives are wrong. Jesus lived as if he trusted that only he and his way would satisfy the Father. This is grace inasmuch as any way to God is grace. It is law inasmuch as there is no other way. It is grace that man is able to be accepted by God at all. It is also grace that the way of it is hidden from us. It is also grace (as well as profound wisdom!) not to let us know how and when we are pleasing

[11] T. W. Manson, *The Sayings of Jesus* (London: SCM Press, 1964), p. 176.

God. In Bonhoeffer's words, "It is grace that we are allowed to please our brother, and pay our debt to him, it is grace that we are allowed to become reconciled with him. In our brother we find grace before the seat of judgement." [12] The gospel of Jesus is both law and grace.

Paul's view of Christianity, inevitably, must in the future be seen in a much wider context. For a long time, Protestantism in particular has acted on the assumption that Paul was our easiest—or only—way into the mysteries of Jesus. Biblical theology's emphasis upon the kerygma was able to show that a recital of the saving acts of God in Christ was the earliest Christian message and the logical preparation for Paul's theology. We must now raise this question: If in fact we no longer need the kerygma to point to the essential mysteries of Christ, must we have the theology of Paul to interpret them? If the kerygma is precisely the point at which we must demythologize, does not the theology of salvation in Paul become even more peculiar, based as it is upon his majestic but probably highly individualistic understanding of the death and resurrection of Jesus, the points of maximum mythical content? Paul regarded "his Gospel" as a very special and peculiar effort designed for a very special and peculiar group, the Gentiles. He was not writing for all time. And he constantly implies that his understanding of salvation was one specially revealed to him to suit his situation, interpret his own experience, and give him a distinctive message for a distinctive task. Contemporary man is no more and no less like such an audience than he is like Jesus' Galilean listeners. Ephesians 3 is a good place to begin studying all this, whether or not Paul wrote it. And all this is a sufficient cause of hesitation when one recent writer,

[12] Dietrich Bonhoeffer, *The Cost of Discipleship* (New York: Macmillan Paperbacks, 1963), p. 146.

having dismissed the notion of revelation, plumps for "salvation" as a preferable overall conception.[13]

Actually, to say that man today can only accept Christ by a *deed*, rather than by faith, is exactly to secure and keep inviolate the magnificent Pauline and Reformation principle that man is not saved by his works, but by grace. For faith, as a positive effort of belief, has become in post-Reformation evangelicalism and Protestantism, and not least in the Reformation-faithful Bultmann schools, indeed a "work," a human "something," a decisive response, a decision. Thus it has become precisely the predictable, manageable, and induceable "thing" that Paul condemned obedience to the Law for becoming. It has become "evil," just as the Law for Paul became evil, because it has become the reason for man's confidence before God and man.

Whereas to say that a man can only accept Christ by a deed is precisely to secure that man recognizes and lives by the unattainable, the unpredictable, the uncontrollable, which is the hidden and only real God. To say that man is saved by a deed is to remove the whole thing from the area of "possibility." The "possibility" of faith in the Protestant or Catholic sense is no problem, for theology has long proved the reasonableness and thus the possibility of faith, with or without divine action. To say that man is saved by a deed is to remove faith into the area where faith alone can truly reside, the area of impossibility, of scandal, of acting in the absence of proof. For to say that man today can only accept Christ by a deed is to put man into the situation of the Gospels, where all that Jesus is and does and says proclaims the hiddenness of the real God, who cannot be dealt with by any man's momentary intention because he has been dealt with all along in

[13] F. Gerald Downing, *Has Christianity a Revelation?* (Naperville, Ill.: Alec R. Allenson, 1964).

every man's life and will be even more if the man becomes a disciple of Jesus.

This is not far from Paul. The origin of his theology of justification by faith seems to have been as much in his own anxiety to prevent any human "boasting" before God (Rom. 3:26-27; I Cor. 1:29) as in any intention to expound a theory of the way in which relationships are established between man and God. The Law had led to a mistaken notion that God's requirement could be predicted, tied down, specified, and thus God's unapproachable righteousness, his unpredictability, the arbitrariness of his hiddenness and his intervention violated. In Christian history, faith has become just what Paul objected to in the Law. It has become a reason for confidence, a cause of boasting. Yet, for Paul all "boasting" was essentially ridiculous, essentially a "joke" (Rom. 5:3; II Cor. 11: 18, 12:9; Gal. 6:14). Paul, for reasons other than those the Gospel writers knew of, has come to identify Jesus with God, so that Jesus shares the unapproachableness of God. If Paul "glories in his sufferings," this is only his little joke; for what suffering could there be, worthy to be mentioned, besides that of Jesus? Paul knows that there must be his deed. He knows too, that his deed is determined by Christ's. His problem is how to relate the two without blasphemy and also with adequate realism.

Another source of skepticism concerning the personal salvation interpretation of Christianity is in the sheer fact of the world as we know it. A view which requires more or less, that the vast majority of mankind is excluded from acceptance, eternal life, salvation, the kingdom, either here or hereafter, is very hard to hold in the face of man's sense of justice or equality. An understanding which excludes the countless millions of Hindus, Moslems, Buddhists, Confucians, Communists, humanists, atheists, idol worshipers, TV-worshipers, capitalists, humanitarians, hedonists, stoics, and ordinary, decent post-Christians is very hard to hold, in the face of man's sense of mercy and "live and let live." A view which essentially requires that all the secrets of life are not only held but are exclusively enjoyed by the curious groups of people who attend churches and claim that they "believe in Christ," but whose life and witness seem to have little connection with the group of Christ's disciples in the New Testament— such a view does not look like the foolishness of God but rather like downright stupidity.

Nor yet does universalism offer any solution. Apart from the difficulty that it looks dangerously like a last-ditch attempt to salvage the old personal salvation theory by saying that all will, in fact, in the end choose salvation, it is also a theory that can only be pressed by emphasizing one side of the gospel, the mercy of God, to the total neglect of another, the judgment of God. In fact, of course, universalism cannot be unequivocably demonstrated from the New Testament, and everyone knows it. The fact that it is so widely believed is because of other factors. It is universalism in which Fritz Buri ends when he claims that the New Testament opens up authentic existence to man, but that we now no longer need this New Testament kerygma myth, as all it means is that now all moments without differentiation are to be received in faith and are "significant." Universalism ultimately and necessarily ends in a denial of any real significance to Christ. What we are arguing for is not universalism, but rather the ultimate significance of those things which have been given significance in Christ.

But what about "eternal life"? The secularizers are usually silent. Gregor Smith breathes not a word. The principal of a theological college wrote to me recently: "You don't say anything about heaven. What is there to believe about an afterlife?" What is there to say, indeed? Does Christ as

Pantocrator mean that we retain belief in a "transcendence over death"? [14]

The Johannine conception of eternal life here and now represents, as Bultmann claims, the first demythologization of the gospel. John took the first unfulfilled eschatological expectation of the early church and demythologized it in terms of a present heaven on earth. Such an idea has obvious comparisons with the kingdom of God or heaven in the Synoptic Gospels and with Paul's conception of life in Christ. Our term "the gift of significance" belongs to the same set of rough equivalents. It has always been difficult to relate any of these biblical concepts to the notions of the end, *eschaton*, or Parousia which the New Testament also contains. If we find it hard to relate the gift of significance to them, we are in good company.

Whatever else they may or may not mean, these expressions about the eternal or ultimate value of that which has been given significance in Christ imply that there exists a situation, state, or existence in which God alone is God, in which the hiddenness of God's deeds within the secular is removed and we can see "face to face."

But what do we see face to face? In Christian tradition, the Jewish eschatological hope has been allied to the Greek notion of immortality and the Pauline notion of bodily resurrection to produce the familiar image of a quasi-physical heaven in which God and Jesus sit on the clouds welcoming individual souls who are thought worthy to be there. This is the picture of the book of Revelation and of countless Christian hymns and liturgies.[15] This picture of individual souls attaining resurrection or immortality has, in the present

[14] Cf. Colin Williams, *Faith in a Secular Age* (New York: Harper & Row, 1966), pp. 86-88.

[15] J. A. T. Robinson, *On Being the Church in the World* (Philadelphia: The Westminster Press, 1962), pp. 129-34.

century, come to include all men of all ages, and apologists assure us that heaven will not be crowded. Aunt Agatha will be there, united with Uncle Bill, sorting out with their grandparents, or even Plato and Lenin, problems which Freud never dreamed of.

Now, as so often, one can only speak as a fool. But this whole picture, so tenaciously held by working-class Western Europeans, most of whom do not attend church, is rejected nowadays by many church members and by even more Christian young people. They reject it because it is simply neither credible nor necessary. As a motivation for Christians or good people, it is discreditable. As a plan for all mankind, in all ages, for all time, it is unlikely. As a special setup for Christians, it is disgusting.

The reason why I must reject it, however, is that it is essentially a picture tied to the limitations of atomistic, individual personalities. What we have discovered in the Gospels is a whole activity of God which is living, dynamic, temporary, not tied to this or that person, but available through Jesus in all kinds of unexpected ways, in all kinds of unexpected combinations, and through all kinds of unexpected combinations, and through all kinds of unexpected people. If there is an eternity or a kingdom hereafter, must it be less than the kingdom here? Must it not rather be a suprapersonal realm, just as it is supraphysical and supratemporal? Must it not be a realm in which is to be found *what* God can use, not merely the individuals who on balance have the "right" notions? Is not one of our besetting shortcomings our constant tendency to personalize everything, whereas God uses *things* dynamically?

In a word, I find it hard to believe that there is an eternal task for me as an isolated individual to fulfill (and any conception of eternity separated from the specific doing of God's will would, again, be less than the kingdom on earth).

But I can occasionally believe that some of the situations, relationships, causes, movements, aspirations, national or group actions in which I have had part and which are larger than "me" might one day be found useful in a realm of depth and meaningfulness, fulfillment, and reality which would be the "kingdom of heaven," and in which all the parts of these things, which seem to have been something to do with Jesus, and many more besides, are seen to be his and blossom into fulfillment. I can sometimes believe that the things that God proclaims as his own in Christ, the things to which in him he gave salvation—that is, the gift of significance—are not *lost,* but are still held dear and lovely and useful.

It is enough.

PART III

Fragments for a New Theology

Chapter 13

A DYNAMIC CHRISTOLOGY

The options open to Christianity in the mid-twentieth century do not seem attractive—any of them. Barth's 1919 bombshell, with all the neo-Reformation "Let God be God" books and all the biblical theology and positivistic theology, has finally begun to wear thin. On the other hand, the desperate measures of the humanists like the Cambridge men, or the secularizers like the World Council of Churches men, can only end up leaving us a Christ-less Christianity and a church which has emptied itself into the world without any source from which the dosage can be repeated by the next generation.

I wish to be allied with neither party. I wish to deny that Barth and the neo-orthodox and the biblical theologians were, in fact, the guardians of the Christian cause. For they only came at the outside—what was indeed the "mythical shell"—of what the *mysterium Christi* was all about. Equally, I wish to deny that the humanists and secularizers have discovered "Christ for our day." For their Christ is a nose without a face, a conclusion without a case, a spirit without an inspiration. The orthodox, revelational Jesus tells us nothing we need to know. The humanist, liberal Jesus tells us nothing we did not know already.

I am attempting to rescue Christ from the orthodox and the liberals and am claiming him for the radicals among Christians and the good men among non-Christians. In this chapter we will take a more careful look around the theological scene and spell out in a little more detail what could be meant by tracing out a "dynamic" theology. And, since Christian theology begins with Christ, that means initially a "dynamic" Christology.

First, we must say something about what is meant and not meant by using the word "dynamic."

The Greek word *dynamis* means power, might, strength, force; also ability, capability; meaning; deed of power, miracle, wonder; resources; power as a personal supernatural spirit or angel; and that which gives power.[1] In a number of these senses, *dynamis* is used by Paul. *Dynamis* is that which the disciples receive (Acts 1:8). According to II Peter 1:3, Christ possesses a *theia dynamis,* a "divine dynamis." The "power of the Lord Jesus" is with the assembled Christians (I Cor. 5:4). It is an attribute of God according to Jesus (Matt. 22:29; Matt. 6:13—the doxology of the Lord's Prayer) and is even a synonym for God (Mark 14:62; Matt. 26:64—"sitting at the right hand of Power"). But even more, it is used in the plural for the miracles of Jesus (Luke 10:13, 19:37; Matt. 7:22, 11:20-23, 13:54, 58), attributed at one point to John the Baptist come to life again (Mark 6:14; Matt. 14:2). Luke 9:1 says that it is *dynamis* (power)

[1] On *dynamis* and *exousia,* cf. W. F. Arndt and F. W. Gingrich, eds., *A Greek-English Lexicon of the New Testament and Other Early Christian Literature* (Grand Rapids: Zondervan Publishing House, 1963), pp. 206-7 and 277-78; also, *Theologisches Wörterbuch zum Neuen Testament,* II; on *dynamis,* W. Grundmann, pp. 286-318; on *exousia,* W. Foerster, pp. 559-71.

and *exousia* (authority) which the disciples are given over evil spirits.

In the apocryphal Gospels the *dynamis* of God descends upon Jesus at baptism and leaves him again at his death. There is, however, no sense at all in the Synoptic Gospels of the *dynamis* of God being some mysterious personal spirit or power that takes possession of Jesus (cf. Acts 8:10!). On the contrary, *dynamis* is always the dynamic action which healing is. It is neither a "stuff" that Jesus holds as a settled possession, nor is it a "power of God from outside" which suddenly descends and then disappears. It is the best word the New Testament can find to describe the action of God in Jesus *at the moment of its occurrence.*

The comparison with the word *exousia*—power in the sense of "capability, might," "authority, warrant"—is instructive. We have already observed, particularly in ch. 8, that Jesus has the *exousia* necessary to perform miracles (*dynameis*) and gets on with the job. In fact, the two words are never used in this justaposition. Jesus has *exousia* to cast out devils (Mark 3:15) and claims *exousia* to forgive sins (Mark 2:10; Luke 5:24; Matt. 9:6). The people conclude from Jesus' teaching that he has *exousia* (Mark 1:22, 27; Luke 4:32, 36; cf. Matt. 7:29). The people praise God for giving such *exousia* to men (Matt. 9:8). The disciples are given *exousia* to tread on snakes (Luke 10:19). The source of this power and authority which Jesus has is the cause of many questions (Mark 11:28-29, 33; Luke 20:2, 8; Matt. 21:23-24, 27): "By what authority are you acting like this? Who gave you authority to act in this way?" (Mark 11:28 NEB.) It is interesting that Jesus answers by implying that he has the same source for his *exousia* as John the Baptist had for his —notably, God. Moreover, Jesus gives his disciples authority (*exousia*) over unclean spirits (Mark 6:7; Matt. 10:1; Luke

9:1). Finally, Matt. 28:18 has Jesus saying that "all authority" has been given to him in heaven and earth.

We must hesitate to dogmatize on the basis of a comparison, but we would not be far out if we said that the word *exousia* usually denotes power in the sense of possession, attitude, total life, while *dynamis* usually denotes power in the sense of expression, miracle, force. The English word "dynamic" is as natural a way of describing the latter as any.

We must now say something about the English word. As a noun or adjective, the word "dynamic" is used, according to the Concise Oxford Dictionary, to differentiate three things in opposition to three others:

(1) Dynamic indicates a *motive* force, in opposition to static.

(2) Dynamic indicates a force *in actual operation*, in opposition to potential.

(3) Dynamic indicates, in the realm of medicine, *functional*, in opposition to organic.

The other meanings are obvious: "active," "potent," "energetic."

Needless to say, I hope, I do not introduce a "dynamic theology" in order to render other theologies by contrast inactive, sterile, or lethargic! Nor yet do I wish to cash in on the technical theological sense of dynamical as implying "of inspiration, endowing with divine power, not impelling mechanically"!

Yet, we need some such title to describe a theology which takes its departure from all theologies of revelation-positivism or incarnation-solidarity-world-as-it-is-accepting (static); or from theologies of eschatology, dialectics, and existentialism (potential); or from theologies of sacramentalism, mysticism, and evolutionism (organic). Additionally, dynamics as "the branch of mechanics that treats of motion in itself, and of the motion of bodies or matter under the influence of forces," or "the branch of any science in which forces are considered" will prove suggestive. The Concise Oxford Dictionary cannot be pressed further! But the main lines of the positions may not be unfairly drawn in this way.

Let us attempt to fill out the significance of theological thinking as "dynamic." First, let us look at the typical ways of thinking of the last and present centuries, particularly as they have been taken over into theology.

Mankind today is becoming less and less accustomed in any sphere of knowledge to static ways of thinking. Not simply from science, but also from sociology, psychology, and economics, man has learned that the human phenomenon and the body politic can no longer be described in terms of scientific, analyzable, atomistic "creation" or "the way things are." Not yet can evolutionary ways of thinking be substituted, as if movement occurred everywhere and at every time in the same direction, and as if man's life could be seen within a historical, lineal perspective. The richly fruitful *Heilsgeschichte* school in theology took over this lineal, not to say evolutionary, view of history, merely adding to it the historical, lineal "end" of the consummation of time.

Nor yet can "organistic" be substituted, for the modern world, despite all its looks toward unity, functions no more as an organism than does society or life itself. The widespread and productive effect of organistic thinking in our day can be seen in the realm of theology. It was the natural product of biological and evolutionary forms of thinking replacing nineteenth-century forms, either monistic, atomistic, or evolutionary. The organistic way of thinking produced a crop of studies in the Roman Catholic Church, particularly on the church and world as the Body of Christ (one thinks of Emile Mersch and Teilhard de Chardin).

What is now needed is for theology to take to itself the dynamistic outlook. The renewed emphasis on the Gospels may well lead in this direction if we have faithfully discerned the kind of claim they make to our thinking. Correspondingly, we may see factors in man's present thought outside theology which might point to the dynamic. The *unpredictability* of modern life is one of modern man's most disconcerting discoveries. The old foundations—moral, social, economic, political, religious—collapse simply under the weight of "happenings." Any kind of theory or science which seeks to make an analysis of man's total situation today must take account of this inconclusiveness, incompleteness, fragmentariness, yet *intensity* of modern life. The sociologists speak of man's confusion at having to function in various capacities in more than one *zone humaine*, or of the pluralism, differentiation, and fragmentation of the structure of his life. We might even risk saying that modern man might see some point of meeting in a theology of the unpredictable, discontinuous, suddenly revelational, adjustable, pragmatic, a theology of discovery, of hiddenness and manifestation, of seeing things falling into place after they have happened (yet not resorting to an Old Testament view of Providence!).

We shall now test out the relevance of a dynamic theology, first with reference to the figure of Christ, then with reference to the doctrine of God.

Much of what we already said in chs. 6–8 will indicate how the "secular" Jesus is always regarded as the "locus" for the actions (miracles, calling, discipleship, forgiveness) and attitudes (parables, discipleship) which the Gospels indicate by a theology of hiddenness and revelation to be authoritative (*exousia*) and filled with power (*dynamis*). It is impossible to separate Jesus from earthly actions, whether or not they have this power. It is also impossible to separate this power from the actions of the secular Jesus. We are not therefore dealing with a "separated" power when we talk of a dynamic Christology. We are talking of the deeds of the secular Jesus.

In order to test the ramifications of this, we may take the interesting and important book of Paul van Buren as a comparison. Initially, there is much that is attractive in van Buren's treatment of Jesus, as when he speaks of a "Christology of call and response," meaning "Jesus [as Son of God] as the obedient bearer of a specific election or commission." [2] Van Buren's effort is directed toward arranging three pieces of the puzzle—the conservative concern with Christology (Barth), the "liberal" concern with a contemporary way of thinking (Bultmann, Ogden) and the logical analysis of theological statements (Wittgenstein). Thus, he comes to the Gospels with gratitude:

If the choice is between "God," however subtly hidden in oblique language, and the man Jesus of Nazareth, the empirically-minded secular "believer" can only choose the latter, for he does not know what to do with theology. Analogical as well as literal language about God makes no sense to him.[3]

The best way out is to talk of man's "blik" instead of his "faith in God." "Christology is the language about Jesus of Nazareth on the part of those for whom he has been the occasion and remains the definition of their 'blik.' " [4] Bultmann tries to say *both* that man's authentic historical (*geschichtlich*) existence is conceptualized in existentialist philosophy, *and* also that Christian faith represents the realization of this only because of the particular historical (*historisch*) event of Jesus. But, as Schubert Ogden says, if the possibility for man's authentic existence is revealed in

[2] Van Buren, *The Secular Meaning of the Gospel*, p. 48.
[3] *Ibid.*, p. 79.
[4] *Ibid.*, p. 91.

a certain philosophy, why do we need Jesus at all? [5] Ogden's conclusions are (1) that we do not need Jesus and that Heidegger will suffice, if man's authentic existence is in fact revealed by an appropriate philosophical analysis; and (2) that we can retain the Jesus-reference if we say that Christian faith is always (not "only") a "possibility in fact," because of the manifestation of the unconditioned gift and demand of God's love in "the event Jesus of Nazareth which, fulfills and corrects all other manifestations." [6]

As van Buren observes, this makes room for faith without Christ, or at least a "Christ" bound up with the historical man Jesus.[7] But it does not meet modern man's need for a statement which has reference to "experienced nonobjective reality"; it does not see that modern man cannot speak of "God acting," even analogically; and yet it does not do justice to the empirical aspect of the kerygma as describing events which happened. Van Buren's own solution is to talk of man's faith as an inexplicable "blik" which becomes "the historical norm" for him:

The man who says, "Jesus is Lord," is saying that the history of Jesus and of what happened on Easter has exercised a liberating effect upon him, and that he has been so grasped by it that it has become the historical norm of his perspective upon life.[8]

As for questions about God, van Buren is clear:

Whatever can be known concerning "God" has been answered by the knowledge of Jesus made available in the event of easter. Whatever "God" means—as the goal of human existence, as the truth

[5] *Christ Without Myth*, p. 112.

[6] *Ibid.*, p. 153.

[7] *The Secular Meaning of the Gospel*, pp. 63-70.

[8] *Ibid.*, p. 141.

about man and the world, or as the key to the meaning of life—"he" is to be found in *Jesus*, the "way, the truth, and the life." [9]

"He who has seen me," says Jesus, "has seen the Father" (John 14:9).

There is much in van Buren's Christology (with which we are alone concerned) which is very attractive and which obviously takes serious account of some of the Gospel evidence in a way not found in most systematic theology. When he speaks of a Christology of call and response, he is saying precisely what we mean by speaking of a "dynamic Christology"—that is, a Christology to be found, witnessed, experienced, and authenticated within the paradoxical deeds, the deeds which both manifest and hide the nature of Jesus as the "anointed one." Moreover, when van Buren emphasizes the nature of faith as the acceptance of a "historical norm of [man's] perspective upon life," this is at least one side of the "faith which works," by which we described discipleship. Finally, we cannot help approving van Buren's reliance upon Jesus for "knowledge" of God, for in fact all we know of God is known through Jesus. Yet this is a "dynamic" reference to God. Inasmuch as Jesus stood in a relation to an act of "anointing" by God, there is some kind of metaphysical reference, but it is a reference which is essentially hidden from all human analysis. It was quite sufficient for men to see the deeds. They do not need to know anything about the relation between Jesus and his Father. What that relationship is, or how it is to be described in terms of titles or anything else, is essentially a mystery in the New Testament. As we saw, it has been our mistake to take our questions in terms of static relationship between Jesus and God—usually put in terms of "Is Jesus the Son of God?" et cetera—whereas it is precisely these questions that

[9] *Ibid.*, p. 147. (Italics mine.)

the New Testament leaves wide open, confining itself to a statement of the power (*dynamis*) at work in Jesus.

Yet, it may be objected, do we not in fact fall back into a "positivism of revelation"? Do we not have to say, ultimately, that you either believe God revealed himself in Jesus or you do not; that you must "pay your money and take your choice"? In the old sense of revelation as "making something clear which was hidden," the answer is obviously "no." If anything that we have said is correct, then it is clearly not a question of man "assessing" the incidents of the Christ-event and concluding that they are or are not "revelation." There is absolutely no way in which such a conclusion can be either justified or not justified. All one can do is to take up an attitude of commitment one way or the other; take the consequences and see what happens. If you take up a positive commitment, then as we have seen, there is a very positive way, a way of discipleship, derived from the works of Jesus. Within it, there might even be "signs following." But there will not be any prior revelation. One writer, indeed, says:

It is very hard to believe that God *intended* to "reveal Himself" (because there is such poor and diverse "knowledge" of Him) or at all *meant* even some lesser insight into his character when He gave us His gift-without-authoritative-explanation in Jesus Christ. But even if nothing of this sort were his intention, could we not watch Him at work and draw some valid conclusions? [10]

Yes, I believe we can, provided we are prepared for the evidence to judge us rather than imagining that we can go back behind the whole Jesus-event and judge it. As soon as we begin to try to "reduce" it, we have lost it. We can be set off by it, but we cannot set it up ourselves. It remains the essential *mysterium Christi* in the light of which all

[10] F. G. Downing, *Has Christianity a Revelation?* p. 278.

things are not "revealed" but a few things become available. We can talk of "revelation" provided that we see that the area within which anything is "revealed" in Jesus is very small: the two years, the parables, the discipleship words, the healings, the prophetic deeds, the passion, the resurrection. As Küng has said:

The whole mystery of Christ is a *mysterium in the strict sense.* Whoever wants to form any concrete images out of all this, or even only an idea *clara et distincta* (especially of the God-man in the bosom of the Father) is on the wrong track to start with.[11]

Küng is speaking of the mystery of Christ's preexistence. What he writes is equally true of his postexistence, his existence with the Father now, his present "living and reigning at the right hand." What he writes is equally true of the whole of New Testament Christology. It is not a statement of "concrete images clear and distinct." It is a statement of *mystery.* The only clues to the mystery are the places where the incognito is broken—almost! They are the places of Jesus' *actions.* That is what we mean by a dynamic Christology.

Hence, if we refuse unequivocally to speak in the older language as if Jesus "revealed" God, then we must be allowed to side neither with "natural" nor "revealed" models for Christology. McIntyre analyzes the "revelational model," as distinct from the two-nature or psychology models for Christology, and shows how christological method is a complex of different methods of approaching the "given," historical, literary-critical, sociological, liturgical, and ethical.[12] This has certainly been the case in the history of Christology

[11] Hans Küng, *Justification,* p. 300.
[12] John McIntyre, *The Shape of Christology* (Philadelphia: The Westminster Press, 1966), pp. 47 ff., 144-71.

and is more or less determined by the nature of the "given"; that is to say, we are given secular incidents (historical) in the form of stories (literary-critical), in the shape of the time (sociological), influenced by what the early Christians made of it all (liturgical), and what they did about it (ethical). That is to say, we do not have in the New Testament a Christology of a settled kind; we have Christology of a *dynamic* kind because it is Christology *that is happening*. Moreover, in discussing the "model," McIntyre follows Ian Ramsey[13] in insisting that it does not mean the same thing as a "title." I would certainly wish to disagree with McIntyre's conclusion when he writes that "the terms in which we understand Christ's character are the ways in which in fact he exists." [14] As he says, christological models are not simply "signposts"—they are realistic and become normative, so that Christian theology builds around them; and also *integratory*, so that life itself and other ideas come to cluster around them. Yet at present there is probably no "model" which will serve our purpose. I have insisted that the whole Christ, who is the "secular Jesus" is the only possible Jesus in the light of whom any age, particularly our own, can open itself to the redeeming strangeness of Jesus.

By speaking of the christological significance of the "whole Christ," I do not wish to imply that here, for the first time, the *totus Christus* comes to his own. I recall the condemnation by von Harnack of those who seek for the first time to give what others do not give—the "whole Christ." [15] But I do mean by this to seek to secure that Christology remains a Christology of the *varied* actions of Jesus and does not become the slave of any one category based upon only a part

[13] I. T. Ramsey, *Models and Mystery* (New York: Oxford University Press, 1964), pp. 4-20.

[14] *The Shape of Christology*, p. 69.

[15] *What Is Christianity?* p. 13.

of his action. Christological reflection to be serious or Christian must take account of what is actually said in the Gospels.

Moreover, it must allow the *manner* in which categories appear there to be determinative and not go rushing off on a tangent, so that the actual Gospel records become no more than illustrations called into the case to confirm an exterior notion.

The theological idea of "representation" is a good example. As frequently employed, this idea suggests that there is a dual representative function of Jesus, as representing man before God and God before man, and that this is supremely shown in the cross.

But, one might ask, is this all there is to it? The representative function of Jesus in the Gospels is to be found supremely in his attitude to his own disciples. He is the first disciple of God, and they must imitate him by learning his words and deeds. They must then act out and repeat the deeds and words before men as his representatives, for in responding to them, the people will be responding to him. But what of the "other end" of the representative function? Here, in the place where Jesus represents man (in this case, again, the disciples supremely) before God, Jesus stands alone. He tries to teach them to pray, but when he departs for a night of prayer, they do not pray with him, and when he prays in Gethsemane, they sleep. Indeed, the whole story of the transfiguration derives its genius precisely from the fact that it is *Jesus alone* who speaks on the mountaintop (Mark 9:4). The disciples wait to see the result. But they do not themselves pray. And despite the additions of Luke and Matthew in the direction of encouraging prayer among early Christians, it seems that Jesus alone was the man who did the praying on behalf of the disciples. The tradition lasts on in the early church, where Jesus "always lives to make intercession for them" (Heb. 7:25), or where the Spirit (who to Paul is identical with the spirit of Christ, as has often been shown) takes up the non-prayer of the disciple and makes it into prayer (Rom. 8:26).

The church has long said that the representative work of Jesus on the cross was "once for all," "unrepeatable." We must now see that the works of Jesus with the Father were also once for all, unrepeatable. There is a residue of suffering left over by the cross, as Paul knew (Col. 1:24). And there is a residue of prayer in Jesus left over by his devotion to God. But the church does not need to be crucified again; it suffices to "take up the cross" (a process, a way; not the deed itself, but the *theatron* of self-denial and service). Does it need to "pray" again, save in a very special sense that is related to the deeds which are the Christ-deeds? [16]

A dynamic Christology, then, seeks to give expression anew to the actual Jesus of the Gospels. It seeks to do so without either falling into the pitfalls of classic Christology based on alien scientific world views, or seeking to codify too much what must remain as mystery. We can hardly hope that this first sketch will meet all requirements for a contemporary Christology. Yet one recalls the tentative feelers of many in this direction. It may be that the messiahship-in-action of Cullmann and Taylor is not utterly foreign to it. "Jesus' own claim concerns what he *does* and what God *does* through him," says Montefiore.[17] "The *identity* of God is somehow bound up with Jesus," says Michalson.[18] "The function of 'Son of God' in the New Testament . . . is more concerned with Jesus' function than with divinity," says

[16] Cf. further my article "Prayer and Modern Man," *The Livingstonian,* I (1966), 18-25; also in my *Here I Stand* (London: Epworth Press, 1967).

[17] H. W. Montefiore, "Christology for Today," *Soundings,* ed. A. R. Vidler (Cambridge: Cambridge University Press, 1962), pp. 147-72.

[18] Carl Michalson, *Worldly Theology: The Hermeneutical Focus of an Historical Faith* (New York: Charles Scribner's Sons, 1967), p. 212.

Hamilton.[19] We seek to take these hints a little further. If messiahship is in action, then so are Christology and discipleship. "What God *does*" is what we mean by speaking of the dynamic present in the deeds. What we mean by "identifying" God with Jesus is that *all* the mysteries are hidden there and that beyond them we do not need to pry; for the dynamic deeds are the hints of all worlds that are. What we mean by "function" is precisely the ambiguous, ambivalent pointing of faith-in-deeds which alone denotes "sonship."

Thus all Christologies now stand even more under the "paradox of grace"—that God uses and discards, that God is here but never localized, that "power" is present but never the source of power—that D. M. Baillie foresaw.[20] The impossibility of analysis or conclusion or title apart from the deeds on which God's blessing rests exposes the long debates before and since Chalcedon to a new stricture, which, we must claim, derives at any rate from one theology of the New Testament.

This then, must be our "christocentric radicalism." [21]

[19] William Hamilton, *The New Essence of Christianity*, p. 77.

[20] Cf. D. M. Baillie, *God Was in Christ* (New York: Charles Scribner's Sons, 1948), esp. pp. 125-32. I should perhaps make it clear that I do not mean by a "dynamic" Christology what Wolfhart Pannenberg means by referring to a "proleptic Christ," a Christ progressively emerging or developing during the New Testament writings—even if our comments on Pfleiderer in chapter 7 acknowledge the historical fact behind this suggestion. To make a theology out of it is another matter.

[21] For a summary, see also my *Here I Stand*.

Chapter 14

A DYNAMIC THEOLOGY

Can theology survive so simple and self-sufficient a Christomonism? I believe it can and must. It is all very well for John Macquarrie to write:

The "death of God" must soon lead to the death of Christianity. If men are adult enough or self-sufficient enough to get along without God, surely they will soon be able to get along without Jesus too. The nostalgic longings of those who once had faith may keep a place for Jesus for a little longer, but soon he too will have to go. If the next generation needs any figure on which to focus its ethical aspirations, it will surely be able to find someone more up-to-date and appropriate than Jesus, for when we consider that his whole life was wrapped up in God, he is not really a very appropriate exemplar for the secular world.[1]

I heartily concur with this critique of the "death of God" theology. But Macquarrie makes the mistake of thinking

[1] *Principles of Christian Theology* (New York: Charles Scribner's Sons, 1966), pp. 143-44.

that the only alternative left to us is to go on with the old supernaturalist frame (admittedly, in his case, in a modern, existential guise, but still very much an "ontology"). But there is a third possibility—that the gospel is about how men can "get along without God" in a metaphysical sense because God is now given to them in the secular; that Jesus' life was "wrapped up in God" because he was wrapped up in the deeds of God; and that the Christian discipleship is living in the way of Jesus *by faith* that underneath are the everlasting arms.

To place Christ thus so firmly in the area of the secular, the historical, and to speak of this as sufficient and essential Christianity does not mean that all talk of "God" is ended, but that all talk of "God" returns completely to the area of faith, where it should always have been. We talk of "God" with confidence as Christians insofar as we have been grasped by the totality of Jesus' view of reality. But on no other grounds, be they of so-called natural theology, metaphysics, personal experience, or deductive reason, can we have confidence in "God" as Christians. "God" thus returns to the place he occupied in the New Testament world, which certainly did *not* have a uniform or constant or firm understanding or concept of "God"—which certainly was a "religious" world, but was religious because God was unknown. What the New Testament adds to this is simply: Indeed, he is unknown because he has willed to hide himself within the world. Naturally, Christian faith will at times speak of "the God and Father of our Lord Jesus Christ" with a confidence based on the appearance of the resurrection in the midst of the life of the Christ-deeds. But, like the resurrection, it will not carry a "demonstration" for the unbeliever, even if, to the discerning, it might carry some hint about the meaning of events in history.

Christian theology thus returns to the attempts, with which

197

it began, to make sense in the light of Jesus. Paul Tillich writes:

The dogmatic work of the early church centers in the creation of the christological dogma. All other doctrinal statements—above all, those concerning God and man, the Spirit, and the Trinity—provide the presuppositions, or are the consequences, of the christological dogma.

And, a little later:

Theology must be free from and for the concepts it uses. It must be free from a confusion of its conceptual form with its substance, and it must be free to express this substance with every tool which proves to be more adequate than those given by the ecclesiastical tradition.[2]

The problem is that the "conceptual form" and the "tool" can so easily provide yet another "presupposition," which becomes a dogma of systematic theology and into which the Christ figure must fit. The notion of the New Being at times seems to become this for Tillich.

John Macquarrie's recent *Principles of Christian Theology* is a good case in point. He sets his own "existential-ontological" understanding of Christianity within the customary framework of philosophical, symbolic, and applied theology, and attempts to construct a system based almost equally on the theology of Karl Rahner and the philosophy of Martin Heidegger. Unfortunately, when he comes to "Christ as the Focus of Being," we have already been told all the characteristics and values of "Being" for which Christ is to be the focus.[3] And, although he says that "we must be prepared to

[2] *Systematic Theology* (Chicago: University of Chicago Press, 1957), II, 139, 142.
[3] *Principles of Christian Theology*, pp. 276-79.

acknowledge a dynamic character in the incarnation," all this leads to is a discussion of "some kind of development" or growth (cf. Luke 2:52) in Jesus' "christhood," with "sinlessness" appearing as the end of a process of development. There is no discussion of the actual evidence of the Gospels, and the figure of Christ is made to fit into an already mapped out ontological scheme, in which "it is at the moment of death that christhood fully emerges" because "God is absolute letting-be, and letting-be is the ontological foundation of love." Therefore, it can only be the case that "just as there is a self-emptying, a kenosis, of God as He pours out Being, so Christ empties himself in the life that is portrayed in the gospels." Now, however much this may seem to illuminate the *Logos* doctrine of John or the kenosis theory of Phil. 2: 5-9, the notion of "self-emptying" is certainly not the conclusion of the Gospels. Even from the point of view of Christology, the matter is far more paradoxical, as Donald Baillie observed. But from the point of view of the story of the Gospels, the theory of "love as letting-be" is simply nonsense. Love in the Gospels is active, healing, forgiving, seeking, saving. The "obedience" of Jesus is not simply submission, but real striving, cooperation, activity. If this does not suit the theological system, then the system must be broken, not Christ broken to fit the system.

Theology must work from Christology, for the claim of Christianity is, essentially, that hidden somewhere in *that* whole existence of the man Jesus is the clue to existence and to whatever God there is and to whatever worlds there are or are to be.

Again, the Christian gospel is not a demonstration that there is a metaphysical or supernatural dimension to life. It is the claim that "all things" are contained in Jesus. This can be only a statement of faith. It cannot be "verified," any more than the significance (as distinct from the historicity) of the events of the gospel can be verified. There is no logical or philosophical way to "prove" that Jesus did or did not walk on the water, or that there is an absolutely static "law of nature" which can only be broken by "supernatural intervention." Equally, there is no way of proving supernatural intervention! T. R. Miles has written:

If criteria cannot be given for recognising the alleged "supernatural agency", the alleged explanation in such terms is vacuous and fraudulent; and if they can be given the agency is not supernatural. It is therefore impossible to accept the natural/supernatural dichotomy without also being caught up in the obscurantism of vacuous explanations.[4]

In fact, the New Testament is not concerned with establishing Jesus as a "supernatural being." When John Robinson claims that "the whole world-view of the Bible . . . is unashamedly supernaturalistic,"[5] he assumes a natural/supernatural dichotomy that is wholly foreign to the Bible, or is at least certainly not a biblical idea. The biblical claim, or assumption, is that God is genuinely to be encountered in the world, whose heights and depths do not require any "supernatural." The images of "God up there," "heaven," and so on, are not supernatural. The Hebrew conception of a three-layer universe was a purely natural one, with God present and ruling each one of them, including hell! (Cf. Ps. 139:8.)

Part of the difficulty with the idea of God is that the arguments for God's existence have always been made as if God were some kind of "thing" or "object" which could therefore be located and whose existence could therefore be reasonably believed. The existentialists made some headway

---

[4] "On Excluding the Supernatural," *Religious Studies*, April, 1966, pp. 141-50.
[5] *Honest to God*, p. 32. Colin Williams calls it "mythical" or "metaphysical," in *Faith in a Secular Age*, p. 78.

out of this by showing that God was essentially other than could be "proved." Tillich and Robinson almost reduce the whole of God to what is to be found beneath human relationships of love; as we saw, this is yet another attempt at "location."

But the location game is up, whether it be played by depth psychology or by sociology or by scientific proof or by analogical philosophy. This is true for two reasons: first, because God is *dynamic;* he is seen in actions, momentarily, as he wills. He has no "continuity"—or at least if he has, he does not show it to us; he only shows his actions. Second, the location game is up because the distinctive truth of Christian revelation is that God is *hidden,* and hidden not in the transcendental, or the Milky Way, or the depths of human personality, or anywhere else as a *settled* location. But he is hidden within the secular, because the secular (men, movements, worlds, sciences, the lot!) is the place where *for man on this earth* God is to be encountered.

Tillich was not right when he spoke of a God beyond God! What is right is that God does not choose to reveal more than is necessary for man to know. What it is necessary for man to know is what there is in Jesus. What there is in Jesus is the revelation of God's dynamic hiddenness within the secular. What it is *not* necessary for man to know has not been told him. "God's presence and his very self" are not revealed; what is sufficient for man now on earth alone is revealed. When Moses asked for God's name, so that the people would obey, he was simply told to say "I AM" had sent him (Exod. 3:14): Get on with the commandments, the things you have been given, and leave God to get on with the rest of the universe! Sufficiently, the claim of Christianity is now that he, Christ, is for man the beginning and ending, the one who is and who was and who is to come (Rev. 1:8); and the

Christian has quite enough to do in getting on with that. The rest is silence.

Whether one needs to use the term "the transcendent" largely depends upon what is meant by the term. Paul van Buren claims that the word itself is not "coinable" or meaningful. It cannot be given any value. Gregor Smith discusses "the death of God" as meaning both the rejection of metaphysic and also nihilism. So Nietzsche's "God is dead" means, as Heidegger says, "the death of God as the name for the realm of ideas and ideals." [6]

If this is the case—and certainly modern man does not use the word much—then it had better go. No "thing" goes if the word "God" goes. "Faith" does not go if the word "God" goes, if faith is, as Gregor Smith says, "what man cannot possess," or "openness to the future," "not knowing where we are going," or, as Harvey Cox has stated:

We meet God at those places in life where we come up against that which is not pliable and disposable, at those hard edges where we are both stopped and challenged to move ahead. God meets us as the transcendent, at those aspects of our experience which can never be transmuted into extensions of ourselves. He meets us in the wholly other.[7]

This in itself, however, can be less than Christian. If the "wholly other" means anything other than the *mysterium Christi*, it is sub-Christian. There is no point in avoiding "delving into each others' depths the way adolescent lovers do" (Cox), if all we do is begin a new search for the "wholly other." The God of Christ is *alongside* mankind. We must be content with what we have—the mysteries of Christ.

Hence, I am bound to say that much of the writings of

---

[6] *Secular Christianity*, p. 165.

[7] *The Secular City* (New York: Macmillan Paperbacks, 1965), p. 262.

the "death of God" theologians, William Hamilton and
Thomas J. J. Altizer, has to be heeded insofar as they draw
our attention to the necessity of removing "God-talk" from
the cultural establishment within which God has been contained, and restoring it exclusively to the realm of faith-
speech on the basis of Jesus. Altizer has written:

If there is one clear portal to the twentieth century, it is a passage
through the death of God, the collapse of any meaning or reality
lying beyond the newly discovered radical immanence of modern
man, an immanence dissolving even the memory or the shadow
of transcendence.[8]

Whether Altizer's holding together of atheism and incarnation will stand the test of time remains to be seen.[9] Certainly
insofar as Christian tradition has presumed to speak of God
as a reality divorced from the mysteries of Christ, the death
of God theology may provide a useful irritant, even if it cannot provide an adequate resting-place. As Bonhoeffer says:

There are not two realities, but only one reality, and that is the
reality of God, which has become manifest in Christ in the reality
of the world. Sharing in Christ we stand at once in both the
reality of God and the reality of the world. . . . Whoever sees Jesus
Christ does indeed see God and the world in one. He can hence-
forward no longer see God without the world or the world without
God.[10]

This means that all talk of the "existence" of God does
not, by any means, cease, for Jesus lived as "the man for
God." But it does mean that much talk about God is *unnecessary*. The basic Christian faith is that if you hold on to

[8] *The Gospel of Christian Atheism*, p. 22.
[9] Cf. T. W. Ogletree, *The "Death of God" Controversy* (Nashville: Abingdon
Press, 1966), pp. 78-84.
[10] Bonhoeffer, *Ethics* (New York: Macmillan Paperbacks, 1965), pp. 197, 70

Jesus, you can stop bothering about anything else—your neighbor, judgment, your future, your world—including God. This is what "seek first his kingdom" means (Matt. 6:33). This is what "all things are yours" means (I Cor. 3:22). The content of Christianity is how man holds on to Jesus, how in him all these other things, and much more, are given to us.

Nor yet does this mean that we abandon all talk of the acts of God. Indeed, it was a firm belief of Judaism that God is not known in "himself," but is known only in his deeds. There is enormous humor in Yahweh's answer to Moses' request for the Almighty's name— "I AM WHO I AM," or, "I WILL BE WHAT I WILL BE" (Exod. 3:13-14).[11] It does mean that we allow talk of the "action of God" to stand under the unexpected, precarious, and unprovable actions of Jesus.

Our relation to God is not a religious relationship to a supreme Being, absolute in power and goodness, which is a spurious conception of transcendence, but a new life for others, through participation in the Being of God.[12]

This "Being of God" is "the Being of Jesus (incarnation, cross, and resurrection)." That is to say, "Everything is concentrated in the life of Jesus; but everything is simultaneously the reality of God. It is in his historicity (in Christ) that God is met in the call of faith."[13] Only the God crucified in Christ is available to us. What God is beyond that, we do not know.

All attempts to cut short the distance between saying, by faith, that God is hidden within the deeds of the secular Jesus, and that God "exists" in some sense other than that which can be deduced from the deeds, must be relegated to

[11] Cf. Eberhard Jüngel, *Gottes Sein ist im Werden* (Tübingen, 1965).
[12] Bonhoeffer, *Letters and Papers*, pp. 237-38.
[13] Gregor Smith, *Secular Christianity*, p. 191.

the area of theoretical, or even philosophical, debate out of which most of Jesus' questioners derived their orientation, but to which Jesus steadfastly refused to give any hint of answer. Is God "father"? The only answer is: Can you live in a world that is beneficent and yourself be beneficent? Is God "king"? The only answer is: Can you live in a world in which the hidden rule of the good, pure, and holy constantly makes its incursion into your existence? Is God "merciful"? The only answer is: Can you look at the deeds of mercy in Jesus and still say there is nothing in it all?

Just because the answers are inconclusive, just because the answers can only "point," just because God is not evident, the Christian proceeds in the abandon, expectation, confidence, and fear which is called faith.

If one persists: Is man alone in the universe or not? (Miguel Unamuno), then the answer is: Of course he is not. But the kind of God to whom Christianity points is a God who has chosen to hide himself. Hence, in the very nature of the case, for all the "signs following" belief which might occasionally even validate it, God can never be proved. "It is in a functional way that man comes into contact with God, that God acquires a meaning in history, especially in the functional history of our time." [14] That is to say, God reveals himself only in the way which we have described as dynamic—in the momentary self-giving, the momentary deed, the momentary action or acceptance. This is not the "whole" of God, we may imagine. But it is what appears. Only the dynamic appears. Christian theology must confine itself to what appears, especially to what has appeared in Christ. It cannot compete with philosophies or philosophies of religion which organize the whole universe into this system or that. It confines itself to faithfully awaiting the God who

[14] Cornelius van Puersen, "Man and Reality, the History of Human Thought," *Student World* (1963), p. 21.

is faithful to Jesus. By "dynamism," we do not mean some kind of dialectic within God between his immutability, consistency, faithfulness, or perfection on the one hand, and his action "in time" on the other.[15] We mean the action of God in Jesus when he says, "This is my Beloved Son; listen to him," when he gives him authority and power, and when he now exerts the same authority and power in the same way in the world today. And by "God," we mean the one whom Jesus hiddenly yet revealingly and sufficiently calls (in Johannine language) "he who sent me" (John 1:33, 4:34), and who, faith proclaims, sends "those who are his" on a like mission in the world today. We do not mean a God who "creatively becomes," but a God who has in Jesus "become creator." [16] If we are pressed for a philosophical ground, we side neither with "I think, therefore I am," nor with "I exist, therefore I am," [17] but with "I act, therefore I am." [18] And God, *a fortiori*, is known neither as concept nor as being, but as action.

---

[15] Macquarrie, *Principles of Christian Theology*, pp. 190-92.

[16] It seems to me, at least on first reading, that the concept of God as "creative becoming" in Schubert Ogden fails precisely on this christological point, unless Ogden has also a concept of a "continuously becoming Christ" which he has not yet developed. If so, he must address himself to our problem! Cf. Schubert Ogden, *The Reality of God* (New York: Harper & Row, 1966), esp. pp. 65-70.

[17] Cf. Rudolph Bultmann, *Jesus Christ and Mythology* (New York: Charles Scribner's Sons, 1958), pp. 45-59.

[18] Cf. John Macmurray, *The Self as Agent* (New York: Humanities Press, 1957), esp. pp. 84-103. By "The Meaning of God as Acting," Bultmann (*Jesus Christ and Mythology*, pp. 60-85) means only what expresses "the existential relation between God and man," which he claims is not merely subjective, psychological experience, but is still only "by His Word spoken here and now" (p. 79). Gerhard Ebeling is still essentially in the same area when he talks of the "dynamic" nature of the God-man relation as existing in "the Word which becomes personal address to the individual" (*The Nature of Faith*, p. 190 ff.). But this Word never *becomes flesh!* I am delighted to see now from Carl Michalson's *Worldly Theology* how he foreshadowed what I call a "dynamic" theology. But I am not sure that he did not see revelation today in word-event rather than incarnation-event.

Chapter 15

JESUS AND THE MEANING OF HISTORY

In this chapter and the next, we shall try to fill in a few more of the gaps in the understanding of the faith that we have described as "dynamic-christological." We shall do so in the present chapter, first, by relating it to current discussions on Christianity and history (section 1, A "Dynamic" Conception of History). Then we shall take up again the debate about existentialism from chapter 11 and suggest the drawing of this category into the sphere of actual life decisions (section 2, An "Ethical" Existentialism). Finally, we shall seek to justify our plan to relate the whole pattern of Christ to the whole of human life and history, by indicating some of the weaknesses inherent either in static understandings of Christian doctrines as related to history, or in taking any one doctrine rather than the total Christ (chapter 12) as the point of entry (section 3, A "Christological" Interpretation of Life).

In chapter 16, we shall discuss some of the current methods of seeking to describe God's present work in history, and seek to justify and expand a little further some, at any rate, of the implications of the "sola-Christologism" of our own position.

(1) *A "Dynamic" Conception of History.* Where, first, does our position place us in relation to current theological understandings of history?

The weakness of biblical theology is that *Heilsgeschichte* got stuck at an atomized view of *Heil* and never really got to *Geschichte* at all. Bultmann even talked of unredeemable, mundane, earthly *Historie,* as over against kairos-filled, redeemed, significant *Geschichte.* Cullmann operated essentially in the same sphere: There was a "history of salvation," which was the area of God's concern, and while (after the mid-point which is Christ), it was intended that all men should be brought into the arena of salvation, the failure of Christian preaching (and sundry moments of truth confronting the church since 1945!) really excluded much possibility of Cullmann's excellent scheme accounting for the dilemmas of contemporary history or church life, even. Bultmann, in reply, stated that the dilemmas were irrelevant, as the point of involvement in the divine activity was a purely personal, existential one. The historical tends to survive in current theological discussion as something of an embarrassment (cf. chapter 4). This is certainly true for Bultmann, and even Cullmann can write:

The scandal for the philosophers of the first century was not a salvation by way of becoming "desecularized," but salvation in connection with history, just as it is for the philosophers of our time.[1]

Cullmann thus claims that the historical is always a problem, but that it is part of the essence of Christianity. Gregor Smith

[1] *Salvation as History,* p. 320.

observes—and he himself does not really remove the problem:

Thus the theory of *Heilsgeschichte* is . . . a story of supreme arbitrariness, of sovereign indifference to the whole sweep of human history, and of a sublime reduction of all that man has done to a handful of selected "moments," objectively certifiable, in the peculiar story of Israel.[2]

Both yes and no, I would reply! It depends on what the "moments" are, and what they are taken to signify in relation to the "whole sweep of human history"—as we shall see. And Gregor Smith has still to give his own meaning to the historical events of Jesus, even if it turns out to be too paradoxical to be practicable.

But is this all there is to say about the historical? I do not think so. When Carl Michalson asserts that theology and faith are essentially "historical," what he means is that they transcend the areas of scientific, historical criticism (*Historie*) and enter the area of meaningful events (*Geschichte*). Faith, he says, like history, will know something only after "a prior interest in knowing," only after "some prior manifestation of knowledge (particularly us shown in significant events)," only in "an act of interpretation (between the historian and the meaning in the history—the *hermeneutic*)," and only in "a risk of judgment." [3] Hence, Michalson insists that faith—or theology—must not presume to be wiser than history, and history must not presume to be wiser than historians! The knowledge of life which is called Christian is essentially an existence based, in faith, on history.

What Michalson almost comes to is what I shall call the *historicizing of the existential*. The existential confrontation

[2] *Secular Christianity*, p. 112.
[3] *Rationality of Faith*, pp. 74-82.

takes place, not simply when the kerygma is proclaimed, but when the whole Jesus-history is set forth. History thus becomes the place where the existential confrontation takes place. History is neither the monotonous rundown of *Heilsgeschichte* nor the existentialist "place of encounter" which otherwise has no interest in history. History is the secular world that God in Christ has claimed for his own. History is the way in which the world works, when it has God in Christ in the midst of it. History is the activity of the secular which may contain the activity of the kingdom. History is the sphere of operation of the contemporary Christ. History is the cloak which conceals the dynamic activity of God, the lines of which appear in Christ. A Christian conception of history is a dynamic conception of history because of the deeds of God which are at once arbitrary (thus "dynamic") and faithful (thus christological).

The *Heilsgeschichte* view of history tends, in fact, to *reduce* the significance of the "once-for-all-ness" of Christ's work by seeing it merely as the historical midpoint—that is, the point out from which the development takes place. This notion of development, as we have already hinted, is not "evolutionary"; yet the comparison with evolution is unavoidable. Hendrikus Berkhof's attempt to build a Christian philosophy of history on the basis of apocalyptic (esp. Mark 13, II Thess. 2, and Revelation) is essentially of like character with a "divine geography" centered on a new Jerusalem.[4] Here, the development merely works backward. Meanwhile, the Bultmann school was doubtless right to object to any scheme of "development," either forward or backward, as Reinhold Niebuhr and others have sufficiently shown. But in the sense of meaning-giving to history by the events of Christ, they were surely wrong.

[4] *Christ the Meaning of History* (Richmond: John Knox Press, 1966).

In the first place, the Christ-events have what we have called a "dynamic" character. They are both discriminate in the *areas* of their manifestation and indiscriminate in the *agencies* of their manifestation. They neither assume a historical rundown (much less buildup) to history's end in the Parousia, nor do they imply a so-called "eschatological" foreshortening of all history in personal encounter and decision. They imply rather that history receives its meaning in the same way that man receives his meaning—by becoming the recipient of the deeds of Christ, by participating in that which can belong to Christ. This cannot happen to history "once," so that things can then jog along in a straight line from that point. Just as with man, so with history, there is need for "taking up the cross day by day." There is need for discipleship within history at every point. Every event in history receives its ultimate meaning insofar as it is reconcilable with the central acts of the whole Christ.

Such a view of history cannot be described by any of the existing labels. The words "repetitionary," or "revelational," or "recurring" would be descriptive, but perhaps we are better remaining with our word "dynamic," since it implies that God in Christ appears within the secular at moments of his choosing, even though these are continuous with the deeds done in Christ. Certainly, I do not wish with Altizer to revise Nietzsche's notion of "eternal recurrence," in the sense of a mystical recapitulation of all things.[5]

Christian revelation is the event whereby God has shown the possibility of significance, of acceptance, latent within any and every human deed or historical event. This brings us near to Barth's conception of an *Urgeschichte,* a primal or eternal history that has its *content* in the life, death, and

[5] Altizer, *The Gospel of Christian Atheism,* pp. 147-57.

211

resurrection of Christ but which forms the basis and hidden meaning of all other history.[6] Such a view, John Godsey has shown,[7] holds together "a view of the history of salvation and the idea of contingent contemporaneity," as does Niebuhr, "thus overcoming both Cullmann's monotonous view of time and Bultmann's volatilisation of history into eschatology." The only difficulty with Barth's view is, as Bonhoeffer observed, that it is too imprecise for man to live by, and so studiously avoids "lo, here" and "lo, there" as to be of little practical use.

Therefore, *history* is the area of the decisions of existence facing both man and historical events. How, more specifically, can man and history meet the hidden significance within the secular?

(2) *An Ethical "Existentialism."* Bultmann *intended* to deliver theology into the realm of "dynamics" when he demythologized the New Testament message and put its essential content into the kerygma, which became real to people in a speech-event. By "speech-event," he intended a method of speaking which *creates* an event, which when repeated *creates* our "present," by simultaneously confronting man with Word, history, and reality. John Macquarrie summarizes this well as follows:

Acceptance of the cross of Christus ($=$ the decision of faith, which is at once renunciation of the world and surrender to God) destroys the idols and overcomes the demons ($=$ abolishes worldly concern and so puts an end to the tyranny of things over men) and thus leads to a sharing in the resurrection of Christ ($=$ brings men into a new life in which they are open for genuine relations with one another and with God).[8]

[6] Cf. Barth, *Church Dogmatics,* IV/3, esp. 116-117.

[7] "History of Salvation and World History," *Drew Gateway,* Winter, 1964, pp. 83-88.

[8] *Studies in Christian Existentialism,* pp. 225-26.

But how, in fact, is this made to happen? By preaching the atonement in any of its classic forms? The experience of growing numbers of Christians denies it.[9] The evidence of the Gospels which we have examined repudiates it. "Acceptance of the cross of Christ" is a way of describing response to the living Jesus. But its ossification within atonement theories is a standing confusion to many (not the stumbling block that Paul intended!—I Cor. 1:23).

Besides, a speech-event, whether of the cross or of the living Christ, cannot do the trick. As we saw in chapter 12, it merely results in a verbal issue, which is not truly "existential." Does not man in fact decide for or against Christ now, as in the days of his flesh, when he is confronted by *a specific decision about what he must do?*

The category of the existential needs to be drawn out to account for the decisions which really confront men—the political, the ethical, the personal. And these are precisely the areas in which the whole Christ of the New Testament operated and operates now. Just as the category of the historical needs to be drawn out into the arena of genuine secular history as the place where the hidden Christ and the hidden kingdom are present (a "dynamic" conception of history), so, too, does the existential need to be applied to the workings of discipleship, the "faith that works" (chapter 10).

For the only place where discipleship can take place is within the concrete decisions of life. And the decisions are *concrete.* They are about "what to do." This is what is meant by an "ethical existentialism"—that every man, be he Christian or non-Christian, responds to parts of the pattern of Christ through the real-life actions that he has to perform.

Do we need the word "existentialism"? Possibly not. Certainly, we do not wish to be involved in the philosophical

[9] Cf. my *Christ and Methodism,* pp. 27-59.

ɨiarangue surrounding it. But it is not a bad word, separated from the harangue. It can mean simply "pertaining to existence," and it carries with it at least some of the undertones of "dynamic." But in using it I would wish to point out that I mean it in a vastly different way from the "existentialists" of the theological and philosophical worlds. We will let it stand, and see whether existentialism can be christologized, after all!

The moment of obedience to Christ is always a "dynamic" moment. It cannot be foreseen. It may well be hidden. But it is the point at which the Christ-deed (revelation-positivism!) strikes through the secular (world-affirmation!) in a concrete moment of decisive action (existentialism of deeds!). I believe that this position would not have been alien to what Bonhoeffer described as "ethics as formation":

Ethics as formation, then, means the bold endeavour to speak about the way in which the form of Jesus Christ takes form in our world, in a manner which is neither abstract nor casuistic, neither programmatic nor purely speculative.[10]

Bonhoeffer says that "concrete judgments and decisions" demanding obedience are the result of this "form of Christ." "Formation comes only by being drawn into the form of Jesus Christ"—and that is to be a "real man." [11]

This, surely, also applies to politics and nations. It is obviously impossible and irrelevant to expect nations to respond to the kingdom's presence as a settled policy. But times do occur when decisions are vital—existential, crucial. Those are perhaps the times when the Christ-events are instructive. All too often, at present, all one hears at such times are pious general principles. But these are the moments when peoples,

[10] Bonhoeffer, *Ethics*, p. 88.
[11] *Ibid.*, pp. 80-81.

movements, nations, classes, groups can "receive what is needful for their salvation" by accepting the implications of incarnation, healing, hiddenness, crucifixion, and resurrection in the policies before them. This is why Christianity is "for the world"—not as a trump card, not as a "told you so," but as a method, a technique, a way, whereby the things seen to be the roots of evil can be removed, whereby the places seen to be the sores can be healed, whereby the state may understand not only what it ought to do, but also what it can expect if it tries to do it.

(3) *A Christological "Interpretation of Life."* I have already hinted, in the references to Macquarrie, that it seems to me that there is great danger and difficulty in taking one part of the Christ-event, and making it the sole point of entry for Christian truth into history or individual lives. The point of entry then was the atonement. One of the findings of the World Council of Churches study on "The Missionary Structure of the Congregation," meeting in April, 1964, is recorded as follows:

The passion and resurrection of Jesus Christ are the Exodus for all men. Now, the whole of mankind is delivered from bondage and brought into covenant with God. By the raising up of the New Man, Christ Jesus, every man has been made a member of the New Mankind.[12]

Not surprisingly, a footnote tells us that there was intensive discussion on this paragraph, and various additions were proposed "therefore he is called to live in faith"; "until man becomes aware of this truth, he does not enter the fullness of Christ"; "but only in faith can he become what in Christ he is."

[12] Thomas Wieser, ed., *Planning for Mission* (London: The Epworth Press, 1966), p. 54.

Each of these comments is instructive. I would not dissent from any of them. But are we not, in truth, making a lot of trouble for ourselves by attempting to use one part of the Christ-event as if it gave the clue to everything whatsoever?

There is a particular temptation to speak of the "cross" in this way. We find Bonhoeffer writing:

Our coming of age forces us to a true recognition of our situation vis à vis God. God is teaching us that we must live as men who can get along very well without him. The God who is with us is the God who forsakes us (Mark 15.34). . . . God allows himself to be edged out of the world and on to the cross. God is weak and powerless in the world, and that is exactly the way, the only way, in which he can be with us and help us. Matthew 8.17 makes it crystal clear that it is not by his omnipotence that Christ helps us, but by his weakness and suffering.[13]

But Matthew 8:17 does not indicate this at all. It is the quotation from Isaiah 53 ("he has borne our griefs and carried our sorrows"), and Matthew uses it to indicate the triumphant ministry of Jesus who "cast out the spirits with with a word, and healed all who were sick" (vs. 16). The whole gospel is not the indication of God's powerlessness at the hands of his world, however relevant this may be in a situation of the church's impotence under persecution. The whole gospel is God's healing and redeeming power in the face of the evil of the world. Human unwillingness to recognize this power and love leads to God's crucifixion. But the cross is only what happens when the ministry is rejected. It is God's activity, not his passivity, which is the dominant theme of the Gospel records of Jesus.

[13] *Letters and Papers,* pp. 219-20. Cf. Dorothee Sölle, *Christ the Representative* (Philadelphia: Fortress Press, 1967), pp. 143-52. Helmut Gollwitzer's able reply, *Von der Stellvertretung Gottes* (Munich: Chr. Kaiser Verlag, 1967) does not explicitly expose this assumed emphasis on God's helplessness in the world, which is now taken for granted in much continental theology.

In another direction, we may see again the danger in taking one strand of the New Testament and making too much of it. The Pauline conception of principalities and powers has recently had a new lease on life through a number of writers.[14] Many of the conclusions these writers draw in applying this notion to modern problems are illuminating and often seem to me correct—particularly those of Albert van den Heuvel. But one must ask whether these conclusions are related to the Pauline notion in anything but the vaguest way. Paul thought of actual cosmic realities. Those who speak of mass media, race, sex, religion, and politics as "powers" are semantically stretching a point. It is highly questionable whether this particular aspect of the New Testament mythical world view can be utilized by contemporary man—or, if it can be, whether anything more is said than would have been said without it. The *positive* side of Christ's work is, it seems to me, a better starting point.

In particular, Romans 13, with its injunction to Christians to be obedient to the higher powers (*exousiai*)—"for there is no authority except from God, and those that exist have been instituted by God" (Rom. 13:1)—has been responsible for more confusion than any other text in the New Testament, particularly on the Continent where it perpetuates the two realms theory of Luther in its most unenlightened form.[15]

As we saw in chapter 13, a dynamic Christology, a Christ-centered theology, does not depend solely upon the Synoptic Gospels. It tries, rather, from the Gospels, to speak of the total acts of God in Christ and utilizes the whole New Testa-

[14] Clinton D. Morrison, *The Powers That Be* (Naperville, Ill.: Alec R. Allenson, 1960); Hendrikus Berkhof, *Christ and the Powers* (Minneapolis: Augsburg Publishing House, 1961); and Albert van den Heuvel, *These Rebellious Powers* (New York: Friendship Press, 1965).

[15] Cf. H. Richard Niebuhr, *Christ and Culture* (New York: Harper & Row, 1956), pp. 149-89; also H. W. Bartsch and W. H. Lazareth in J. C. Bennett (ed.) *Christian Social Ethics in a Changing World* (New York: Association Press, 1966), pp. 59-77; and pp. 119-91 respectively.

ment as a continuation of them. A christological interpretation of life is one which sees itself as caused and determined by Christ's acts. To become a Christian is to be content that the acts whereby all men in fact may become significant should appear in our mortal bodies. Our life itself (personal, moral, social, political) is the place of the ongoing work and activity of Christ himself in his world. It is the situation within which faith becomes possible. It is the area where discipleship takes place. It is the area in which the committed disciple acts out his own response to Christ's own acts in the gospel.

We conclude, therefore, by bringing together the elements of the picture of discipleship as the continuation of Jesus' work (ch. 10, sec. 3), and seeing them in the light of the fivefold work of the contemporary Christ (the five "alls" of ch. 11). This is the Christian "interpretation of life."

(i) Christ is where his deeds are done; and the disciple is called to *service*.

(ii) Christ is where his ministry of healing and redemption is continued; and the disciple is called to *healing*.

(iii) Christ is being dealt with, ministered unto, or rejected, in the person of others—hidden within the secular—and the disciple is called to *recognition*.

(iv) Christ is on the cross; and the disciple is called to *suffering*.

(v) Christ is ruling his universe, both openly and secretly; and the disciple is called to *indication*.

The five aspects of discipleship are the disciple's obedience within this pattern, the description of the points at which he may enter into his Lord's continuing work. They become the points of application for the disciples who seek to share in "what God is doing in the world."

Chapter 16

WHAT IS GOD DOING IN THE WORLD?

Probably no question has evoked more discussion in the
World Council of Churches and elsewhere over recent years
than the question of God's action within the modern world.
As the New Delhi Assembly declared:

The Christian must always recognise that Jesus Christ is the Lord
of History and he is at work today in every nation of the world in
spite of, and through, the ambiguous political, economic or social
structures and actions in any given country.[1]

Of course, there are dangers in this attitude. There is the
danger of equating well-justified efforts and most welcome
events directed toward social progress directly with the
promises of Christ. To proclaim them as the deeds of Christ
means "allowing the social efforts and events which occur
in a social revolution to decide what is the gospel or the

[1] *New Delhi Report*, ed. W. A. Visser't Hooft (New York: Association Press,
1962), p. 102.

presence of Christ."[2] H. H. Wolf has recently criticized this in the light of the Barmen Declaration of 1934, with its thesis: "We repudiate the false teaching that the Church can and must recognise yet other happenings and powers, personalities and truths as divine revelation alongside this one Word of God, as a source of her preaching." In a reply, M. M. Thomas objects to Wolf's implied division of history into secular history and salvation history, and argues that "the creaturely and redemptive promises of Christ" must have political implications, and that it was a *religious* perversion against which Barmen was directed.

Of course, there are good reasons for the desire to remain "uncommitted." As Jan Lochman has pointed out, history is both the *hominum confusiones* and also the *dei providentia,* and both demand that one refuses to make history a "source of revelation," through which we discover our faith, for that can only lead to absolutization of our own position: "and where I absolutise myself, I necessarily regard others as demoniacal."[3] But there is no conception that when we are, in Bruce Reed's words, "discerning the activity of God in a concrete situation," we, in fact, have anything to *take* to the situation as a "contribution," apart from generalities.[4] And so, we might well ask again: Is there a Christian contribution? Is the Christian simply to wait and see? Are the "marks of Jesus" in fact what he has to look for, or does he just listen with "complete openness"? This is the question which divides christological from anthropological perspectives. Basically, one feels that the church's uncertainty in action in the present century is due to an *inadequate Christology.* Far too often the total work of Christ is ignored,

[2] H. H. Wolf, "Christ at Work in History," *Ecumenical Review,* January, 1966, pp. 1-20.

[3] "Die Bedeutung geschichtlicher Ereignisse für ethische Entscheidungen," *Theologische Studien* (Zürich: EVZ-Verlag, 1963), LXXII, 17.

[4] Cf. Bruce Reed, in *Christian Social Ethics,* ed. John C. Bennett, pp. 115-18.

and the cross and resurrection alone cited as the starting point of the church's existence and action. This is particularly true of van Leeuwen and Bonhoeffer; indeed, Harvey Cox seems to be the only exception, and it is much to be regretted, as we shall see, that his basic case proves christologically eccentric.

Discussions with professionals in a number of spheres convince me that it is the *self-authenticity* of the Christian's word which is the only thing that the professional asks us about. He does not expect us to be any wiser than he is in dealing with the complicated issues of his own sphere. What he does ask, when we presume to intrude our "Christian presence," is not simply that we be "with him" in the problem in question—that is taken for granted by his presence and ours, by the facts to which we must listen, by the situation which creates our common concern—but whether or not we have anything to contribute. I recall vividly a conversation on the matter of disarmament with one who is now a member of the present British government. The conversation took place at one of the early meetings of the Conference for Christian Approaches to Defense and Disarmament. "What I want to ask you all," he said, "is what you have to contribute to these problems from your Christianity."

Again, we are told repeatedly that modern man only thinks *inductively*. It is obviously true. The world of science, indeed, the world in general for four hundred years, has worked on the assumption that truth and action must be discovered by deduction from available facts. If the Christian contribution is a set of laws, revealed axioms, or static concepts, then, of course, there is little future for any Christian contribution. The only possibility is for an *inductive* procedure which begins with openness to the facts. All I wish to add is this: Christian faith *means* that *one of the elements with which we have to do is the hiddenness of God in the secular in the image of Christ.* Thus we start, not as John Robinson says,[5] from "the primacy of persons and personal relationships," but with the primacy of the mysteries hidden in the world; not with Christianity as "humanism within a mystery," but as mystery hidden within humanity—the mystery of the whole Christ, the secular Christ. This does not mean that we see clear programs for every issue. Perhaps theology in this respect is like poetry: "Poetry does not move us to be just or unjust, in itself. It moves us to thoughts in whose light justice and injustice are seen in fearful sharpness of outline." [6] The "fearful sharpness of outline" applies, says Bronowski, to all creative thought. Does it not apply to theology? Are there no "fearful sharpnesses of outline" which the Christian has to contribute?

Thus, the essential question for Christian ethics must always be: Where is Christ? If we begin with the question: What is God doing in the world? our answer is determined by our Christian faith. God is doing whatever Christ is now doing—and Christ is doing all the things he "began to do" in the days of his flesh. Ernst Käsemann once described miracles in this way:

Miracles in the New Testament are . . . a self-manifestation *in the sphere of our corporeality* of the God who addresses us; as such, they are intelligible only to the believer and do not remove the offence given to the unbeliever.[7]

What is God doing in the world? Manifesting himself in the sphere of our corporeality by means of the Christ-events.

[5] *Christian Morals Today* (Philadelphia: The Westminster Press, 1964), pp. 42, 46.
[6] J. Bronowski, *Science and Human Values* (New York: Harper & Row, 1964), p. 81.
[7] *Essays on New Testament Themes* (Naperville, Ill.: Alec R. Allenson, 1964), p. 53.

And the standing temptation to the modern secular Christian is that he tries to bend over backward to "remove the offence given to the unbeliever."

But is this too narrow? It will doubtless appear too narrow for the secularizers who strain to be "with it" in a moment of technological and ideological confusion such as the world is now passing through. To tie the "Christian element" so firmly to specific *parts* of history is surely to acquiesce in the all too familiar ghetto attitude of Christians, and to make a philosophy of history out of it. Surely, they would complain, the significant parts of history are not only those where ministry, self-sacrifice, hidden self-identification, and new life through death take place! Yet this objection can always be made to any understanding of existence based on the Christ-events. There is, in Käsemann's words quoted above, no way of removing the "offence given to the unbeliever" by the "self-manifestations of God in the sphere of our corporeality." All that the Christian can do is to make what he can of the Christ-events. This Bultmann brilliantly achieved in the direction of the individual, but in so doing he surrendered to a particular philosophy and also neglected the sphere of action in history. What I am attempting to do is to take the Christ-events *in the place where they occurred,* notably the world, and to ask what was meant *for the world* when the New Testament tells us of the mission of Jesus and of the twelve, which involves "all men" and "all things." This I take to be an understanding of an inner dynamism within the world which is the hidden God.

Clearly, this inner dynamism which is the hidden God cannot be "located." It can only be understood "in faith." But faith has the whole ministry and work of Christ to go on. It is this that points, that proclaims, that "reveals," that *works.* It is this to which the disciple (whether the twelve or Paul) points when he talks of revelation and reconciliation.

The Christian's task is to look for the marks of Jesus, the lineaments of his total work, in the midst of all life. Here we finally part with the secularizers. Gregor Smith movingly writes:

[Faith's] only way is to carry in the body, that is, in the historical existence in the world which it both maintains and endures, the marks of Jesus. But these marks are not the sacred stigmata of the kind the crowd longs to see and touch. They are the marks of absolute openness, which is absolutely engaged with the historical possibilities of the hour.[8]

But how can the Christian be absolutely open when the "marks of Jesus" already tell him so much? This is the point we have to raise against so much in this debate.

Christian "social witness," like Christian discipleship, is simply *participation in Christ's hidden lordship*. The disciple's task is to live in a world over which Christ is already the only Lord and simply to bear witness to this by his deeds. The lordship of Christ is both over the church and over the world. His exaltation to the right hand of God (Phil. 2:9) proclaims him *kyrios* (Acts 2:35-36). At present, this lordship is visibly exercised only in the church (Eph. 3:10-21), but it shall be manifest to all the world in the end, for everything has been put in subjection under his feet (Eph. 1:22). Within this situation of Christ's lordship, the disciple must proclaim Jesus' triumphs (I Peter 2:9), for "the grace of God has dawned upon the world with healing for all mankind" (Titus 2:11 NEB). Hence, the disciple follows his Lord into the heavens (Rev. 14:4).

Christianity, then, is God's method of providing the possibility of acceptance for the whole of the *kosmos*. It is his means of providing for the secular world as such to hide

[8] *Secular Christianity*, p. 200.

within it the kingdom, as such to be accepted, as such to be part of the messianic, that which can have God's blessing resting upon it.

If the Christian believes that he has, indeed, a way whereby the world must live, then he will play out the implications of this within secular structures. He will herald the presence of what he looks for wherever he sees it. And what he looks for is the continuation of Christ's work of healing, exorcism, instruction, and recognition. And if he finds that this commitment costs him dear, he will recall that this commitment cost Jesus the cross. The good news of Christianity is that you cannot separate an understanding of yourself or your world from that understanding which has already been given to them by Jesus Christ. And to be a Christian is to be prepared for this to be manifest in your mortal body. Christianity is all that understanding of existence which is hidden in Christ, and the appearance of *this* is what the world is waiting for, from the church and from us, today.

It is, in fact, at this crucial, christological point that Harvey Cox's thrilling and fascinating book reveals itself as ultimately eccentric and impossible. Starting with just such a basis in the Gospels as that for which we have argued, Cox takes the categories of kerygma, diakonia, koinonia, and exorcism and applies them to the modern world. We must confine our comments at the moment to a single point which, in fact, gives the lie to the whole thesis. Cox identifies the kingdom of God with the secular city by suggesting that the "idea of the secular city supplies us with the most promising image by which *both* to understand what the New Testament writers called 'the Kingdom of God' *and* to develop a viable theology of revolutionary social change." [9]

Cox seeks to meet three objections to this identification. First, that "whereas the Kingdom . . . is the work of God

---

[9] Cox, *The Secular City*, p. 110.

alone, the secular city is the accomplishment of man." He rightly replies to himself that "if Jesus personifies the Kingdom of God, then the elements of divine initiative and human response in the coming of the Kingdom are totally inseparable." *But* this does not mean that the secular city can now stand in the place of the kingdom of God as the concern of the contemporary Christian, as Cox is arguing. His second point is that the "Kingdom . . . demands renunciation and repentance, [while] the secular city requires only skill and know-how." He quotes some admirable statements about the need for repentance in the Gospels and then merely asserts that "life in the emerging secular city entails precisely this kind of renunciation"—without giving any proof whatsoever.[10] Family, possessions, reputation, and future are the things by which the secular city in fact lives. It is utter nonsense to say that the city demands their renunciation!

Cox's third imaginary objection is that "while the Kingdom of God stands above and beyond history (or exists in the heart of believers), the secular city is fully within this world." But the argument here becomes mere shadowboxing. Cox refers to the eschatology "in process of realizing itself" (*sich realisierende Eschatologie*) school, as between the "future" school and the "already come" school of eschatology, and remarks that "we live today in a world where what the New Testament writers described as the coming of the Kingdom *still* occurs." But this is naïvely and without argument identified with the "objectively new social situation." This identification is never proved either from the theological or the

---

[10] *Ibid.*, p. 113. Cox seems unaware still of the methodological impossibility here. Cf. *The Secular City Debate*, ed. Daniel Callahan (New York: Macmillan Paperbacks, 1966) pp. 193-94. I think his "sectarian" stance there is New Testament: but for different reasons, related rather to the revelation-centered character of Christian ethics. Cf. Paul L. Lehmann, *Ethics in a Christian Context* (New York: Harper & Row, 1963), esp. pp. 45-101.

sociological point of view. The kingdom which "still occurs" is merely the city.

If Cox's seminal study lands us in a position where the christological categories have no distinctive value or relevance any longer, this only points up the exciting possibilities for a theology of God's action in history and society which would be completely based on the actions of God in Christ, and which would seek to discern the techniques whereby God may be assumed to be still working as he worked in the Christ-deeds in the New Testament. This would mean careful and patient experimentations with the christological categories in the various areas of modern secular existence, which would attempt to delineate the actions of the "dynamic Christ," who is our contemporary now. Referring back to the five "alls" of chapter 11, we could imagine that such experimentations would seek to describe the "dynamics of Christ's action in the world now," perhaps in some such way as this:

(1) The *all things made by Christ* as pointing to the way of *Christology* and the dynamics of Christ in human existence, as the new being of humanity foreshadowed in Jesus, differentiating itself from all attempts to abandon Christology for mere humanism.

(2) The *all men found in Christ* as pointing to the way of *healing* and the dynamics of Christ in human morality, as the "new morality" of the kingdom, differentiating itself from all bogus "new moralities."

(3) The *all things held together in Christ* as pointing to the way of *hiddenness* and to the dynamics of Christ in society, as the hidden presence of the issues of discipleship within secular situations, differentiating itself from all theories of mere "progress."

(4) The *all things find their end in Christ* as pointing to the way of *suffering* and to the dynamics of Christ in politics, as the way whereby the techniques of identification and

crucifixion operate, differentiating itself from either "mere expediency" or "pure witness."

(5) The *all things are yours* as pointing to the way of *resurrection* and to the dynamics of Christ in Christian discipleship and devotion, as the personal renewal of Christ visible in the actual pattern of existence "in Christ," differentiating itself from theories of Christian discipleship based purely on either vicariousness or mysticism.

This is a first sketch of the task to which I turn in "The Dynamics of Christ." [11]

---

[11] Cf. meantime the works cited in footnote 3 of the Preface.

EPILOGUE

The Death of God and the Resurrection of Christ

If our day is a day of the "death of God," how can it also be a time for a rediscovery of Christ? Is not Christ the "man for God"? How, without the framework of God, can we ever think we can live by Christ?

This is, doubtless, the crucial question to be raised against any contemporary attempt to live by "christomonism," to speak of "faith" as holding to the Christ-deeds in the absence of proof, to understand Christian existence sufficiently as praying to a God not personally known: "Only look on us as found in him." What is to be said in reply?

First, that we must be allowed our own understanding of the "death of God." As a statement concerning the existence or nonexistence of a supreme being, the statement is nonsense. Whatever God there was, there is, and will be forever. What is meant by the death of God, at least in my view, can only be that the God of all *establishments* (intellectual, churchly, experiential, philosophical, scientific) is dead. Not simply has the "God of the gaps" gone, but also the God who is the underlying "sense" of a cosmos, the "truth" at the heart of the universe man discovers. The "omnipotent" God, the "God of providence," the "just" God has disappeared in the debates about war, suffering, purpose, redemption. The "omnipresent" God has disappeared in the debates about science, universalism, and pantheism. The "personal" God has disappeared in the post-Freudian debates about anthropology and psychology and sociology.

Let that God go—not merely because he is an embarrassment to the Christian intellect in the modern world, *but because he is not the God and Father of our Lord Jesus Christ.*

The God and Father of Jesus was "believed in" by the first Christians not because, as Jews or pagans, they had always had a God hanging around, but because God raised up Jesus. Or, rather, because Jesus had been raised up, there was now something to be said about God. There had been a breakthrough. Everything else followed. If God had raised up Jesus, then he must approve the things that belong to Jesus. If God had raised up Jesus, then there was something to shout about concerning a world in which that could happen (kerygma!). If God had raised up Jesus, he would so quicken also the men who stood with Jesus now on earth. *It was because of the resurrection of Jesus that the earliest Christians believed in the existence and relevance of God.*

This carries with it the essentially Christian corollary: The God in whom the Christian believes is that God who stands behind Jesus. And in a day of uncertainty about the absolute, the eternal, the metaphysical, the Christian is the one who stands simply on the ground: I believe in the One who believes in Jesus. I have faith in the One who has faith in Jesus. And along the way I am prepared to labor on the assumption, justifiable only along the way, that there is grace, power, energy (*dynamis*) available for the deeds on which God's blessing rests, just as these were given to Jesus, on whom God's blessing rested and now rests forever. I stand on the ground that is given me to stand on in Christ. I exist in a world in which deeds done with hands like mine to men like me carried the imprimatur, the anointing, of God—and I know that as Jesus' "Christology" is in action, my action also is in Jesus and thus my "acceptance." I exist in the body of disciples which heals in the world, just as Jesus' "kingdom" overflowed for the needy. I enter into every relationship, encounter, experience, with joy, with *hilaritas*, with expectation, with curiosity, with fear, with hope—for the kingdom is hidden, and the parables are about me. I repent, have faith, take up the cross all together, new every moment; for the same Jesus calls me to "the faith that sweetly works by love." I look for the resurrection of the body, the ultimate acceptance before my very eyes, and even finally before the eyes of the whole creation, of those things which in me are lost with Christ. And I proclaim in acted parable, in attitude, in deed and word the significance shown in the Christ-events which now resides in the midst of the world. The God and Father to whom I look is thus, alone and sufficiently, the God who receives Jesus' actions, the God who is hidden in Jesus' miracles, the God who is pointed to in Jesus' parables, the God who is "Father" to the whole mystery of discipleship, salvation, and significance, whereby men become part of a new family and sing a new song.

There is a second thing to say about the "death of God." Is it not the God of the middle-aged who is dead? Is it not the God of Western culture past its prime of life, stirring enviously in the emotions of its past? The God of the "classic" period of Western culture was indeed the God of whom we have said: He is not the God and Father of Jesus—the God we caricatured as "establishment," omnipotent, omnipresent, personal. Today, we need to listen to the God of the rising cultures of Africa, Asia, of communism and nationalism, of revolution and hope and promise. Can Camus, Freud, Koestler, Eliot, even Auden give us a God of young men, or even the young man Jesus? Why do others speak hope to other men, while we Christians can only hear hopelessness?

If Bonhoeffer was right that man in our time has newly got the key of the door, has just "grown up" to manhood after adolescence, has just emerged not to maturity but to the hope and promise of twenty-one, with career, courtship, business, acceptance all still ahead of him, why do we linger with the God of a dead culture, the God of the middle-aged? Does not Jesus point us, despite all our theological problems, to the One who gives us anew in him the key of the door? We can only learn whether its source is "he who is" if, like Jesus, we take it.

INDEX OF SCRIPTURE

INDEX OF AUTHORS

235

INDEX OF SUBJECTS

BIBLIOGRAPHY

Note: Books named in the text in their American editions are here given their British publishers.
Where not otherwise noted, place of publication is London.

AINGER, G. J., *Jesus our Contemporary*, SCM Press, 1967.

ALTHAUS, P., *The So-Called Kerygma and the Historical Jesus*, Edinburgh: Oliver & Boyd, 1959.

ALTIZER, T. J. J., *The Gospel of Christian Atheism*, Collins, 1966.

——, and Hamilton, William, Radical Theology and the Death of God, Indianapolis: Bobbs-Merrill, 1966.

ANDERSON, H., *Jesus and Christian Origins*, Oxford University Press, 1964.

ARNDT, W. F., and GINGRICH, F. W., eds., *A Greek-English Lexicon of the New Testament*, Cambridge University Press, 1957.

BAILLIE, D. M., *God was in Christ*, Faber and Faber, 1948.

BARR, J., *Semantics of Biblical Language*, Oxford University Press, 1961.

BARTELS, R. A., *Kerygma or Gospel Tradition?*, Minneapolis: Augsburg Press, 1961.

BARTH, K., *Church Dogmatics*, Edinburgh: T. & T. Clark, 12 vols, 1949–65.

——, *The Humanity of God*, Collins, 1966.

BARTSCH, H. W., ed., *Kerygma and Myth*, SPCK, 1953.

BENNETT, J. C., ed., *Christian Social Ethics in a Changing World*, SCM Press, 1966.

BERKHOF, H., *Christ the Meaning of History*, SCM Press, 1966.

——, *Christ and the Powers*, Minneapolis: Augsburg Press, 1961.

BEST, E., *The Temptation and the Passion: The Markan Soteriology*, Cambridge University Press, 1965.

BLACK, M., *An Aramaic Approach to the Gospels and Acts*, Oxford University Press, 1954. 3rd edition awaited.

BONHOEFFER, D., *Letters and Papers from Prison*, SCM Press, 1953. 2nd edition, 1967.

——, *The Cost of Discipleship*, SCM Press, 1959.

——, *Christology*, Collins, 1966.

——, *Ethics*, Fontana Books, 1964.

BORNKAMM, G. *Jesus of Nazareth*, Hodder & Stoughton, 1960.

BRAUN, H., *Spätjüdisch-häretischer und frühchristlicher Radikalismus*, Tübingen, 1957, 2 vols.

BULTMANN, R., *Theology of the New Testament*, SCM Press, 2 vols., 1952, 1955.

——, *History of the Synoptic Tradition*, Oxford: Basil Blackwell, 1963.

——, *Jesus and the Word*, Nicholson & Watson, 1935.

——, *Jesus Christ and Mythology*, SCM Press, 1958.

BURKHILL, T. A., *Mysterious Revelation*, Oxford: Basil Blackwell, 1961.

CALLAGHAN, D., *The Secular City Debate*, New York; Macmillan Paperbacks, 1967.

COX, H. E., *The Secular City*, SCM Press, 1965.

CRANFIELD, C. E. M., *The Gospel According to St Mark*, Cambridge University Press, 1959.

CULLMANN, O., *Christ and Time*, SCM Press, 1952.

——, *The Earliest Christian Confessions*, Lutterworth Press, 1949.

——, *The Christology of the New Testament*, SCM Press, 1964.

——, *Salvation in History*, SCM Press, 1967.

DAVIES, W. D., *The Setting of the Sermon on the Mount*, Cambridge University Press, 1964.

DIBELIUS, M., *From Tradition to Gospel*, Nicholson & Watson, 1935.

DODD, C. H., *The Parables of the Kingdom*, Nisbet & Co., 1936.

——, *The Apostolic Preaching and its Developments*, Nisbet & Co., 1935.

DOWNING, F. G., *Has Christianity a Revelation?*, SCM Press, 1964.

EBELING, G., *The Nature of Faith*, Collins, 1964.

——, *Theology and Preaching*, Collins, 1966.

EDWARDS, D. L., ed., *The Honest to God Debate*, SCM Press, 1963.

FARRAR, A., *A Study in St. Mark*, Faber & Faber, 1951.

FIEBIG, P., *Die Gleichnisreden Jesu*, Tübingen, 1912.

FINDLAY, J. A., *Jesus and his Parables*, Epworth Press, 1950.

FUCHS, E., *Studies in the Historical Jesus*, SCM Press, 1964.

FULLER, R. H., *Interpreting the Miracles*, SCM Press, 1963.

——, *The New Testament in Current Study*, SCM Press, 1963.

——, *The Foundations of New Testament Christology*, Lutterworth Press, 1965.

GALLOWAY, A. D., *The Cosmic Christ*, SCM Press, 1955.

BIBLIOGRAPHY

GERHARDSSON, B., *Memory and Manuscript: Oral Tradition and Written Transmission in Rabbinic Judaism and Early Christianity*, Lund, 1961.

GODSEY, J. D., *The Theology of Dietrich Bonhoeffer*, SCM Press, 1960.

GOLLWITZER, H., *Von der Stellvertretung Gottes: Christlicher Glaube in der Erfahrung der Verborgenheit Gottes*, Munich, 1967.

GOGARTEN, F., *Demythologizing and History*, SCM Press, 1955.

GRANT, F. C., *The Earliest Gospel*, Nashville: Abingdon Press, 1943.

HAMILTON, W., *The New Essence of Christianity*, Darton, Longman & Todd, 1966 (*see also under* Altizer).

HANSON, A. T., ed., *Vindications*, SCM Press, 1966.

HARNACK, A. VON, *What is Christianity?*, Williams & Norgate, 1901.

HEALEY, F. G., ed., *Prospect for Theology: Essays in Honour of H. H. Farmer*, Nisbet & Co., 1966.

HIGGINS, A. J. B., *Jesus and the Son of Man*, Lutterworth Press, 1964.

——, ed., *New Testament Essays: Studies in Memory of T. W. Manson*, Manchester: University Press, 1959.

JENKINS, D. E., *The Glory of Man*, SCM Press, 1967.

JEREMIAS, J., *The Parables of Jesus*, SCM Press, 1955; 2nd ed., 1962.

——, *The Prayers of Jesus*, SCM Press, 1967.

JÜLICHER, A., *Die Gleichnisreden Jesu*, Tübingen, 2 vols., 1888–89.

JÜNGEL, E., *Paulus und Jesus*, Tübingen, 1962.

——, *Gottes Sein ist im Werden*, Tübingen, 1965.

KÄHLER, M. *Der sogennante historische Jesus und der geschichtliche biblische Christus*, Berlin, 1896, reprinted 1961.

KÄSEMANN, E., *Essays on New Testament Themes*, SCM Press, 1964.

KITTEL, G., ed., *Theologisches Wörterbuch zum Neuen Testament*, 7 vols., Stuttgart, 1932–66.

KNOX, J., *The Death of Christ*, Nashville: Abingdon Press, 1958.

——, *The Church and the Reality of Christ*, SCM Press, 1962.

——, *Myth and Truth*, Carey Kingsgate Press, 1966.

——, *The Humanity and Divinity of Christ*, Cambridge University Press, 1967.

KRAMER, W., *Christ, Lord, Son of God*, SCM Press, 1966.

KÜNG, H., *Justification*, Burns & Oates, 1964.

KÜNNETH, W., *Theology of Resurrection*, SCM Press, 1965.

KÜMMEL, W. G., *Promise and Fulfilment*, SCM Press, 1957.

LADD, G. E., *Jesus and the Kingdom*, SPCK, 1966.

LEANEY, A. R. C., *The Rule of Qumran and its Meaning*, SCM Press, 1966.

LEHMANN, P. L., *Ethics in a Christian Context*, SCM Press, 1963.

LOEN, A. E., *Secularization: Science without God?*, SCM Press, 1967.

LOHMEYER, E., *Das Evangelium des Markus*, 16th ed., Berlin, 1963.

MACLEOD, G. F., *Only One Way Left*, Iona Community, 1956.

MACMURRAY, J., *The Self as Agent*, Faber and Faber, 1957.

MACQUARRIE, J., *Studies in Christian Existentialism*, SCM Press, 1965.

——, *Principles of Christian Theology*, SCM Press, 1966.

MANSON, T. W., *The Teaching of Jesus*, Cambridge University Press, 1931, 2nd ed., 1943.

——, *The Sayings of Jesus*, SCM Press, 1949.

MANSON, W., *Jesus the Messiah*, Hodder & Stoughton, 1944.

MASCALL, E. L., *The Secularization of Christianity*, Longmans, 1965.

MCINTYRE, J., *The Shape of Christology*, SCM Press, 1966.

MICHAELIS, W., *Die Versöhnung des Alls*, Berne, 1950.

MICHALSON, C., *The Rationality of Faith*, SCM Press, 1964.

——, *Worldly Theology: The Hermeneutical Focus of an Historical Faith*, New York: Charles Scribner's Sons, 1967.

MINEAR, P. S., *The Kingdom and the Power*, Philadelphia: The Westminster Press, 1950.

MITCHELL, J., ed., *The God I Want*, Constable, 1966.

MOLTMANN, J., *Theology of Hope*, SCM Press, 1967.

MORRISON, C. D., *The Powers that Be*, SCM Press, 1960.

MOULE, C. F. D., *The Phenomenon of the New Testament*, SCM Press, 1967.

MUNBY, D. L., *The Idea of a Secular Society*, Oxford University Press, 1963.

NEWBIGIN, J. E. L., *Honest Religion for Secular Man*, SCM Press, 1966.

NIEBUHR, H. R., *Christ and Culture*, New York: Harper & Row, 1956.

NIEBUHR, R., *The Nature and Destiny of Man*, Nisbet & Co., 2 vols., 1941–43.

NINEHAM, D. E., *Saint Mark*, Pelican Gospel Commentaries, 1963.

——, ed., *Studies in the Gospels: Essays in Memory of R. H. Lightfoot*, Oxford: Basil Blackwell, 1955.

OGDEN, S. M., *Christ Without Myth*, Collins, 1962.

BIBLIOGRAPHY

OGDEN, S. M., *The Reality of God, and other Essays*, SCM Press, 1967.
OGLETREE, T. W., *The "Death of God" Controversy*, SCM Press, 1966.

PANNENBERG, W., *Grundzüge der Christologie*, Gütersloh, 1964.
——, ed., *Offenbarung als Geschichte*, Göttingen, 1961, 2nd. ed. 1963.
PEACHEY, P., ed., *Biblical Realism Confronts the Nation*, New York: Fellowship Publications, 1963.
PELZ, W., *God is No More*, Victor Gollancz, 1963.
PERCY, E., *Die Botschaft Jesu*, Lund, 1953.
PERRIN, N., *Rediscovering the Teaching of Jesus*, SCM Press, 1967.
PFLEIDERER, O., *The Early Christian Conception of Christ*, Williams & Norgate, 1905.
PHILLIPS, J. A., *The Form of Christ in the World*, Collins, 1967.
PILSCHNEIDER, O. A., *Christus Pantocrator: Vom Kolosserbrief zur Ökumene*, Berlin, 1962.

RAHNER, K., *Theological Investigations*, Darton, Longman & Todd, 4 vols., 1961–66.
——, *The Christian of the Future*, Burns & Oates, 1967.
RAMSEY, I. T., *Models and Mystery*, Oxford University Press, 1964.
RICHARDSON, A., *An Introduction to the Theology of the New Testament*, SCM Press, 1958.
——, *Religion in Contemporary Debate*, SCM Press, 1966.
ROBINSON, J. A. T., *Jesus and his Coming*, SCM Press, 1957.
——, *On Being the Church in the World*, SCM Press, 1960.
——, *Honest to God*, SCM Press, 1963.
——, *The New Reformation?*, SCM Press, 1965.
——, *Exploration into God*, SCM Press, 1967.
ROBINSON, J. M., *The Problem of History in Mark*, SCM Press, 1957.
——, *The New Quest of the Historical Jesus*, SCM Press, 1959.
——, and COBB, J. B., *New Frontiers in Theology*, New York: Harper & Row. Vol. 1: *The Later Heidegger and Theology*, 1964. Vol. 2: *The New Hermeneutic*, 1965. Vol. 3: *Theology as History*, 1967.
ROOT, H. E., et al., *Religion and Humanism*, BBC Publications, 1964.
ROUTLEY, E., *The Man for Others*, Derby: Peter Smith, 1964.

SCHNIEWIND, J., *Das Markusevangelium*, Göttingen, 1953.
SCHWEITZER, A., *The Quest of the Historical Jesus*, New York: Macmillan, 1957.

SCHWEIZER, E., *Lordship and Discipleship*, SCM Press, 1960.

SMITH, R. G., *Secular Christianity*, Collins, 1966.

——, ed., *World Come of Age*, Collins, 1967.

SÖLLE, D., *Christ the Representative*, SCM Press, 1967.

STAUFFER, E., *New Testament Theology*, SCM Press, 1955.

——, *Jesus and his Story*, SCM Press, 1960.

TAYLOR, V., *The Gospel according to St. Mark*, Macmillan & Co., 1952.

——, *The Names of Jesus*, Macmillan & Co., 1953.

THORNTON, M., *The Rock and the River*, Hodder & Stoughton, 1965.

TILLICH, P., *Systematic Theology*, Nisbet & Co., 3 vols., 1953–64.

——, *Biblical Religion and the Search for Ultimate Reality*, Nisbet & Co., 1956.

TINSLEY, E. J., *The Imitation of God in Christ*, SCM Press, 1960.

TÖDT, H. E., *The Son of Man in the Synoptic Tradition*, SCM Press, 1965.

TORRANCE, T. F., *Theology in Reconstruction*, SCM Press, 1965.

VAN BUREN, P., *The Secular Meaning of the Gospel*, SCM Press, 1963.

VAN DEN HEUVEL, A., *These Rebellious Powers*, SCM Press, 1965.

VAN LEEUWEN, A.TH., *Christianity in World History*, Edinburgh House Press, 1964.

VERMES, G., *The Dead Sea Scrolls in English*, Penguin Books, 1962.

VIDLER, A., *Twentieth Century Defenders of the Faith*, SCM Press, 1965.

——, ed., *Soundings*, Cambridge University Press, 1962.

VINCENT, J. J., *Christ in a Nuclear World*, Crux Press, 1962, 2nd ed., 1963.

——, *Christ and Methodism: Towards a New Christianity for a New Age*, Epworth Press, 1965.

——, *Here I Stand*, Epworth Press, 1967.

——, *The Working Christ*, Epworth Press, 1968.

VON OPPEN, D., *Das personale Zeitalter*, Christen in der Weld, VII, 1960.

WEISS, J., *Paul and Jesus*, New York: Harper & Row, 1909.

WIESER, T., *Planning for Mission*, Epworth Press, 1966.

WILDER, A. N., *Otherworldliness and the New Testament*, SCM Press, 1955.

BIBLIOGRAPHY

WILLIAMS, C. W., *Faith in a Secular Age*, Fontana Books, 1966.

WREDE, W., *Das Messiasgeheimnis in den Evangelien*, Göttingen, 2nd ed., 1913.

ZAHRNT, H., *The Historical Jesus*, Collins, 1963.

Note

There is a useful annotated bibliography of synoptic studies up to 1965 in Perrin, *Rediscovering the Teaching of Jesus*, pp. 249–66. Van Ouwerkerk's article (*see* page 46) performs a like function for the secularism literature, while J. M. Robinson's article, "Revelation as Word and as History", in *Theology as History*, pp. 1–100, summarises much of the contemporary German theological debate.

F. H. Borsch, *The Son of Man in Myth and History* (SCM Press, 1967) and M. D. Hooker, *The Son of Man in Mark* (SPCK, 1967), arrived too late to be considered here. The relation of a "Dynamic" Theology to Process Philosophy was too large an issue to be opened here.

(*October*, 1967.)